VERMONT KITCHENS REVISITED

A Collection of Recipes
Compiled by the Women of
the Cathedral Church of St. Paul

VERMONT KITCHEN PUBLICATIONS
Burlington, Vermont
1990

ISBN: 0-9627253-0-7

Proceeds of the sale of this book will go to support
the good works of the Cathedral Church
of St. Paul, Burlington, Vermont.

1st printing — August 1990-5000 copies
2nd printing — September 1991-4000 copies
3rd printing — April 1994-4000 copies

Printed in Vermont by Queen City Printers Inc.

Artist: Margaret Parlour
Design and production: David Robinson
Keyboarding: Marna Mráz
Typesetting: Peter Kriff

Contents

The Cathedral of St Paul
Burlington, Vt.

About the Artist

A native of Buffalo, N.Y., Margaret Parlour attended UVM in the 1940s, returning to Vermont in 1981 to make her home in Panton. She has studied with a number of Vermont artists, including Francis Colburn, Hendrik Glaeser, and Lawrence Goldsmith; her work has been exhibited in the Burlington, Middlebury, and Rutland areas. About herself she says: "Much of my life has been lived in rural, often remote, places, and as time allowed I have painted and studied. Life's greatest joys, for me, are found in interaction with the natural world and in the search to understand our relationship to it. The truths I find there are most often revealed in the work of creating art."

Acknowledgments

The committee wishes to express its gratitude for the outpouring of recipes submitted to it. Those appearing in this book have been tested, edited, and in cases of duplication or overlap, merged where appropriate.

Special Thanks to:

The Rev. Bruce H. Jacobson, former Dean of the Cathedral Church of St. Paul, for his enthusiasm and support in the beginning stages of this project.

Janet Rood, whose faithful concern for our predecessor, *Out of Vermont Kitchens*, and interest in a new book combined to provide the spark that got us underway.

Lyn Rothwell, nurse practitioner with special focus on nutrition, who read this manuscript from a "heart healthy" point of view and gave us many valuable tips and ideas.

Rux Martin, Food Editor of *Harrowsmith Country Life* Magazine, who generously contributed both her excellent editorial eye to our manuscript and her unfailing support to the committee.

The Rev. Canon Michael Dugan, who took the time and trouble to collect recipes on his trips to Portugal for the Diocese of Vermont.

Mrs. Warren Hamm, who graciously agreed to translate our Portuguese recipes into English.

Cookbook Committee

Johanna Thomas, General Chairman
Marilyn Stout, Editor
Patricia McDonald, Testing and Marketing
Sally Swenson, Co-chairman, Marketing
Janet Rood, *Out of Vermont Kitchens*

Priscilla Dugan
Grace Hill
Gayle Jacobson
Lyn Rothwell
Carol Walters

Introduction

We published our first cookbook, *Out of Vermont Kitchens*, in 1939. The world and the small corner of it that is Vermont were much different then, and yet some things stay the same. Not only is that first book still in print and going strong, but the values it represents—fresh ingredients cooked with pleasure and creativity for family and friends—are with us still today.

Vermont itself is a blend of old and new, a study in contrasts. It is still a rural state with many small, family dairy farms and sugarbushes, but in recent years an influx of new residents from "down country" has brought us new life and richness with their interest in organic gardening, sheep raising, and the production of a variety of cheeses and home-cooked products now sold far beyond our borders. While treasuring our wonderful maple syrup and dairy products, we also welcome the addition of a broadened range of produce, ethnic foods, herbs, and spices to our shelves.

Vermont is a place of distinct seasons and sometimes harsh climate, but always of outstanding beauty. Much of our life continues to involve church suppers, town fairs, country auctions, and rigorous outdoor activity, along with a penchant for self-reliance and the homegrown. Our more recent neighbors have often settled here because they too love these simpler pastimes and values. Those of us fortunate enough to live here wouldn't be any other place.

So come into our kitchens. Sit down and browse awhile through our recipe files and well-thumbed favorites. Then join us around the table to share a dish that, in the universal spirit of kitchen creativity, you have made your own.

Appetizers

Thetford Center, Vt.

Marinated Brussels Sprouts

A surprisingly wonderful accompaniment to cocktails—pretty to look at, healthy to eat, easy to do. The marinade is also good with mushrooms; use about a pound of small-to-medium, firm white ones with this amount of liquid.

2 (10 ounce) packages frozen Brussels sprouts
½ cup tarragon vinegar
½ cup salad oil (half olive oil, half other)
1 clove garlic, minced—or more, if you wish
1 tablespoon sugar
Salt to taste
Hot pepper sauce, to taste
1 tablespoon sliced scallions
Dried tarragon to taste—start with ½ teaspoon and add to taste

Cook and drain Brussels sprouts, being careful not to overcook. When they are tender but still firm, remove from heat and plunge into cold water to retain their green color.

Combine remaining ingredients, mixing well. In a bowl, mix marinade and sprouts and let stand at least 8 hours, stirring often.

For your heart's sake, substitute low-fat cottage cheese, whirled in the processor and thinned with yogurt or milk, for sour cream in your favorite dip recipes. Or add your own flavorings to the cheese mixture, such as garlic salt and dill weed, Parmesan cheese and minced garlic, grated Cheddar cheese and garlic, minced parsley and scallions. It is an infinitely variable base for dipping.

Steamed Grape Leaves

If you have a grape arbor in your back yard, you can pick your own leaves for this recipe. Otherwise, look in your grocery or specialty food store for preserved ones.

6 tablespoons olive oil
1 cup finely chopped onions
⅓ cup uncooked long-grain white rice
¾ cup water
½ teaspoon allspice (optional)
½ teaspoon salt
2 tablespoons (or more) pine nuts
Freshly ground black pepper
2 tablespoons dried currants
40 grape leaves
2 tablespoons cold water
Lemon wedges
Yogurt

Heat 3 tablespoons olive oil over moderate heat until haze forms. Add onions and cook until transparent. Add rice and stir to coat with oil. Add ¾ cup water, salt, and pepper, and bring to a boil. Cover tightly and simmer until all liquid is absorbed—about 15 minutes. Heat 1 tablespoon oil in a small skillet and cook pine nuts until golden. Add along with currants to rice.

If you use fresh leaves, bring 2 quarts water to boil in a large pot. Drop leaves in and immediately turn off heat. Let leaves soak for 1 minute, then drain and plunge in ice water. Spread on paper towels to dry.

If you used preserved grape leaves, drain them, rinse well in cold water and dry on paper towels.

Working on a flat surface, put 1 tablespoon filling on dull side of leaf and fold over 4 times, starting with the stem end. Line bottom of heavy 3-quart casserole with 10 leaves and stack the stuffed leaves, seam side down, on top in layers. Sprinkle with 2 tablespoons oil and the cold water. Place casserole over high heat for 3 minutes. Reduce heat to low and simmer,

4

tightly covered, for 50 minutes. Uncover and cool to room temperature. Garnish with lemon wedges and serve with yogurt for dipping. Makes about 28 pieces.

For an attractive change from the usual, serve unpeeled apple slices instead of crackers with cheese. Alternating green- and red-skinned slices makes an appealing presentation.

Crispie Cheddar Rounds

One of our all-time favorite recipes. Easy, tasty, versatile—a roll of this dough in your freezer will have you well prepared for unexpected guests.

1 stick (¼ pound) butter or margarine at room temperature
1 cup grated sharp Vermont Cheddar
1 cup flour
1 cup Rice Krispies

Preheat oven to 350 degrees. Put first 3 ingredients in bowl of food processor or mixer and process until well mixed. Transfer to bowl if necessary and work in Rice Krispies by hand. Form dough into rolls about 1½ inches in diameter and chill for a while.

Slice into thin rounds and place on ungreased cookie sheet. Bake for about 10 minutes, but keep an eye on them—the time can vary from oven to oven. Makes about 40–50 pieces. Store in a covered tin and crisp briefly in the oven before serving.

Variations: You can add variety here by adding one or some of the following—tabasco, caraway seed, dry mustard, steak sauce.

Veggie Snacks

1 bunch broccoli, broken into flowerets
1 head cauliflower, broken into flowerets
2 cups carrot pieces
2 cups mushrooms—whole if small, halved or quartered if large

Dressing:
2 cloves garlic, crushed
¾ cup vegetable oil
½ cup wine vinegar
2 teaspoons cider vinegar
2 teaspoons sugar
1 teaspoon salt
1 teaspoon dry mustard
1 teaspoon basil
½ teaspoon pepper
Dash of nutmeg, if you like

Whisk dressing ingredients together and combine with vegetables in a bowl.
Marinate overnight, stirring now and then.

Marinated vegetables are versatile. They are not only good with drinks but make interesting additions to salads and attractive garnishes on the dinner plate. Consider keeping a jar of one or another in your fridge.

6

Artichoke Bites

The donor says, "These aren't done until they're carried somewhere!"

2 packages artichoke hearts, drained and rinsed if canned
2 cloves garlic, peeled and split
2 tablespoons grated onion
2 tablespoons chopped parsley
Pinch ground coriander
$1/16$ teaspoon dried oregano
$1/16$ teaspoon dried basil
3 tablespoons Roquefort cheese
$1/3$ cup olive oil
$1/3$ cup white vinegar

Mix all ingredients and let stand at least 2 hours. Serve with toothpicks.

Walnuts, pecans, or peanuts are made more interesting for snacks by stirring in warmed butter in a heavy skillet until almost toasted, then seasoned with cayenne, chili powder, tamari, or other seasonings of your choice. Drain on paper towels.

Hot Artichoke Dip

1 can (14 ounces) artichoke hearts or bottoms, drained
1 cup freshly grated Parmesan cheese
8 ounces cream cheese at room temperature
$1/2$ cup good-quality mayonnaise
$1/4$ teaspoon minced garlic (a small clove)
$1/2$ teaspoon dried dill

Place the artichoke hearts in food processor and chop coarsely. Add half of each of the remaining ingredients and process until smooth. Scrape mixture into a shallow oven-proof dish (about the size of a 10-inch pie plate). Repeat procedure with remaining ingredients and add to mixture in the oven-proof dish. Smooth top with spatula and bake at 350 degrees until hot and bubbly—about 15 minutes. Serve immediately with bread sticks.

Antipasto Party Spread

3 carrots very finely diced
3 large onions, finely chopped
3 green peppers, finely chopped
2 large cloves garlic, minced
½ cup olive oil
2 (8 ounce) cans tomato sauce
2 teaspoon Worcestershire sauce
1 teaspoon vinegar
3 (7 ounce) cans white tuna, drained and finely flaked
4 sweet gherkins, finely chopped
1 (24 ounce) bottle ketchup
15 peppercorns
4 bay leaves
2 (8 ounce) cans mushrooms, drained and chopped
1 small can ripe olives, sliced

Steam carrots until tender, about 5 minutes. In a good-sized, heavy saucepan, sauté the onions, peppers, and garlic in the oil. Do not let them brown. Add tomato sauce, Worcestershire, and vinegar. Simmer for about 5 minutes.

Add all remaining ingredients and simmer for 15 minutes. Mixture will be thick and chunky. When done, pour into hot sterile jars and seal. Makes about 4 pints and keeps well in the refrigerator for several months.

To serve, bring to room temperature and pass with assorted crackers.

Common crackers, which are dense, bland, and crunchy, were first made in Montpelier, Vermont, in 1828. They filled cracker barrels for 153 years. An authentic but smaller version is again available. Split the puffy cracker to use many ways: spread with cheese or jam, toast in the oven as a base for hors d' oeuvres, crush to use in stuffings, or layer for scalloped oysters.

Mediterranean Summer Vegetables

2 medium eggplants
2 peppers (1 green, the other red or yellow)
1 celery stalk, chopped
1 large tomato, chopped
2 tablespoons chopped fresh parsley
2 tablespoons olive oil
2½ teaspoons cider or wine vinegar
2 garlic cloves, pressed or chopped
Salt and cayenne, to taste

Preheat oven to 400 degrees. Roast the eggplants (skin pierced several times with a fork) and peppers right on the oven rack. Line oven bottom with foil to catch the juices. Peppers will blister in about 25 minutes. Remove from oven, cool 5 minutes, peel, seed, and chop. Eggplant will take about 50 minutes. When soft, scoop out the pulp, chop finely and discard skins.

While the vegetables are roasting, combine everything else in a bowl. Add the chopped eggplant and peppers, then add salt and cayenne to taste. Marinate in the refrigerator at least 2 hours or, even better, overnight. Serve with pita triangles.

Spinach Balls

2 (10 ounce) packages frozen chopped spinach, thawed and drained well
2 small onions, finely diced
¾ cup melted margarine or butter
½ cup grated Parmesan cheese
2 cups seasoned stuffing mix
½ teaspoon pepper
1 teaspoon garlic powder, or to taste (or mince 1 clove garlic)

Mix all ingredients well. Let stand ½-1 hour, then form into 1-inch balls. Bake on greased cookie sheet for 15 minutes at 350 degrees.

Serve warm with mustard sauce (page 269) for dipping.

These may be frozen. Spread on cookie sheets, freeze, then put in plastic bag. They keep well for quite a while and can be reheated in the oven when you wish to serve them.

10

Tofu-Yogurt Dip

Particularly wonderful with fresh vegetables—try fresh, young asparagus, steamed to crispy-green tenderness and cooled in the refrigerator.

Depending on the amount you want:

1 part tofu
1 part plain yogurt
1 part light mayonnaise
1 tablespoon Dijon mustard
1 tablespoon coarse, grainy mustard

Blend tofu and yogurt in food processor until smooth—this may take time, so don't despair. Add mayonnaise and mustards.

Chill for at least 1 hour in the refrigerator until it thickens. Pour into a pretty bowl, garnish with paprika and surround with an array of fresh vegetables.

Possible dippers, steamed lightly where appropriate, for both good taste and eye-appeal:

Asparagus spears
Artichokes
Broccoli flowerets
Brussels sprouts
Cauliflowerets
Cherry tomatoes
Endive
Green beans
Green onions
Kohlrabi slices
Mushrooms
Radishes
Purple cabbage
Peppers of every hue
Snowpeas
Turnips
Zucchini

Hummus

Middle-Eastern flavors, heart-healthy versatility. This is one of those wonderful recipes that could easily become a staple—serve with veggies or on pita triangles with drinks, as part of a salad plate, as a sandwich base. This recipe makes over a quart of hummus—keep some in the fridge or in the freezer. You won't be sorry.

For a basic hummus, place in the bowl of a food processor:

3 (15 ounce) cans chick-peas, drained (reserve some of the liquid)
3 large cloves garlic, coarsely chopped
¼-½ cup tahini (available at health food stores)
2 tablespoons tamari
Juice of two medium lemons
Tabasco, to taste
1 teaspoon or more ground cumin
Salt, if desired

Process until smooth, adding reserved chick-pea liquid if needed. Taste for seasonings; adjust as you wish.

For extra interest and texture:
In 1 tablespoon vegetable oil, sauté until tender

1½ cups finely chopped onion (3 medium onions)
¾ cup finely chopped carrot (1 medium carrot)
4-5 cloves garlic, finely minced (omit garlic from above recipe)

When vegetables are lightly browned and tender, combine by hand with chick-pea mixture. You may also add chopped parsley for added color and flavor.

Store in refrigerator in container with tight-fitting cover.

Hot Crabmeat Dip

1 (8 ounce) package cream cheese, softened
1 tablespoon chopped onion
½ teaspoon horseradish (or more if you want it)
1 can crabmeat, drained
Slivered almonds

Sauté slivered almonds (about ¼ cup should do it) in butter until golden. Set aside.

Mix remaining ingredients, place in a greased oven-proof dish, and sprinkle the sautéed almonds on top. Bake at 350 degrees for 20 minutes. Serve in a chafing dish or on a hot tray—best kept warm.

Note: The basic cream cheese-crabmeat base may be flavored with other seasonings if you prefer. You might try:

1 teaspoon dry mustard
2 teaspoons seasoned salt
Tabasco to taste

For a delightful nibble, keep plastic bags of grapes in your freezer.

Hot Crab and Spinach Dip

2 (10 ounce) packages frozen chopped spinach
1 bunch scallions
¼ cup butter or margarine
½ clove garlic, minced
Salt, pepper, tabasco, to taste
2 (8 ounce) packages cream cheese
8 ounces crabmeat
¼ cup grated Parmesan cheese
Milk

Thaw spinach and squeeze all liquid from it. Sauté onions in butter or margarine and mix with spinach and seasonings.

In a double boiler, melt cream cheese, and add spinach mixture, Parmesan, and crabmeat. Combine and thin with milk to desired consistency.

Serve in a chafing dish with corn chips for dipping.

If you have a can of salmon and some cream cheese and need a quick spread, mix them together with capers and a bit of anchovy paste. Good with dark bread or crackers.

Hot Chipped Beef

8 ounces sour cream
8 ounces cream cheese
8 ounces high-quality mayonnaise
Chopped scallions, to taste
3 (4 ounce) packages chipped beef, diced

Preheat oven to 325 degrees. Combine sour cream, cream cheese, and mayonnaise, blending until smooth. Add remaining ingredients, combining well. Pour into an oven-proof dish from which you can serve and bake for 45 minutes. For variety add minced green pepper and/or chopped pecans. At Christmas add red pepper too, for seasonal colors.

Mimi's Cheese Spread

2 (8 ounce) packages cream cheese, softened to room temperature
1 cup Cheddar cheese, grated
¼ pound Roquefort or bleu cheese
1 teaspoon Worcestershire sauce
1 tablespoon grated onion
1 tablespoon white wine, sherry, or brandy
1 clove garlic, minced

Mix all ingredients in food processor or mixer—let it beat for 10 minutes or so to thoroughly combine everything. Then refrigerate or freeze. Good served on wheat or rye crackers.

This spread makes a wonderful gift. You can pack it in crocks, or form into balls which you then roll in a mixture of chopped parsley and chopped walnuts. The recipe makes lots!

Tuna Mousse
(Mock Salmon)

This dish can be served with crackers as an hors d'oeuvre, or as a light lunch accompanied by salad and bread. It freezes well.

1 can tomato soup, undiluted
2 envelopes unflavored gelatin
1 (8 ounce) package cream cheese, softened
1 cup mayonnaise
½ cup lemon juice
Dash tabasco sauce
¾ cup finely diced celery
1 medium onion, grated
1 (12½ ounce) can water-packed white tuna, drained and flaked

Heat soup to boiling and add gelatin, stirring with a whisk after each envelope to dissolve. Let this mixture cool to room temperature.

Meanwhile, in a large bowl, combine cream cheese, mayonnaise, lemon juice, and tabasco, beating well. When smooth, add tomato mixture, vegetables, and tuna; mix well.

Pour into a well-greased 1 or 1½ quart mold (vegetable spray or mayonnaise works well for greasing), cover closely and refrigerate until set. Or freeze, if you plan to keep it any length of time. Makes 1 quart.

Shrimp Butter

½ cup soft butter
1 (3 ounce) package softened cream cheese
1 can (4½ ounce) tiny shrimp, drained
2 teaspoons lemon juice
¾ teaspoon onion salt
¼ teaspoons paprika
Dash ground red pepper or tabasco, to taste

Cut butter and cream cheese into chunks and place in food processor with metal blade. Add remaining ingredients and process until blended, scraping the sides of bowl as needed. Chill for 1 hour. Allow to soften; spread on crackers. Makes 1½ cups.

Substitute plain low-fat yogurt for sour cream in dips and salad dressing.

Crab Canapés

1 (7½ ounce) can crabmeat, drained
1 tablespoon chopped scallion
1 cup shredded Swiss or Cheddar cheese
½ cup mayonnaise
¼ teaspoon curry powder
½ teaspoon salt
1 teaspoon lemon juice
1 package butterflake refrigerated biscuits
1 can water chestnuts, sliced

Combine all ingredients except biscuits and water chestnuts. Separate each biscuit into 3 pieces, flatten each piece into a circle, and put a dollop of crab mixture on top of each. Top with a slice of water chestnut and bake for 12 minutes at 400 degrees on a greased baking sheet. They should be puffy and golden brown.

Curried Cheese Paté

An elegant and unusual centerpiece for your next cocktail party—and a good addition to a buffet table. Can be made ahead and refrigerated.

2 (8 ounce) packages cream cheese, softened
2 cups grated sharp Cheddar cheese
6 tablespoons sherry
½ tablespoon Worcestershire sauce
2 teaspoons curry powder

Cream cheeses with remaining ingredients. Line an 8-inch cake pan with plastic wrap, or lightly grease an 8-inch springform mold. Fill with cheese mixture, cover with plastic wrap and chill 4 hours. May be frozen at this point—bring to room temperature before proceeding.

Unmold cheese on a large platter. Garnish with the following, in order given:

1 jar chutney
½ cup chopped unsalted peanuts
½ cup chopped green onions
½ cup grated unsweetened coconut

Serve with crackers of your choice.

For an emergency cheese spread, mix in a food processor a piece of Cheddar cheese with enough dry sherry to be creamy and enough Worcestershire sauce to give it bite.

Beer Batter Halibut Mutineer

From an Alaskan relative who serves these tidbits with drinks to guests. We think they are just as good here in Vermont.

1 cup white flour
½ teaspoon garlic salt
1 teaspoon paprika
½-¾ teaspoon creole seasoning
Salt and pepper, to taste
1 can beer
Halibut—or any other firm fish such as salmon or scallops in an amount to serve your numbers
Clean oil for deep-frying

Mix dry ingredients together in medium-sized bowl and add beer to make a batter about the consistency of pancake batter.

Cut fish into 1-inch cubes and thoroughly coat them with batter. Deep-fry in clean, hot oil for 1–2 minutes or until the batter turns a light golden brown.

Drain pieces on paper towels and serve with toothpicks. Pass with any cocktail sauce of your choice.

Chicken Niblets

2 whole chicken breasts, skinned, boned, and cut in half
¼ cup soy sauce
2 tablespoons rice vinegar
2 teaspoons sugar
6 scallions, chopped
1 jar roasted red peppers, drained and chopped

Flatten breasts to about ½ inch thick and trim all fat. Combine the soy sauce, vinegar, and sugar. Add chicken and marinate for at least an hour in the refrigerator.

Remove chicken from marinade, drain it, and place it on a heat-proof platter. Put the platter on a flat steamer rack in a skillet in which there is about 1 inch of boiling water. Cover chicken with chopped scallions and peppers.

Cover the pan and steam chicken about 5 minutes, or until firm. Let chicken cool and then cover it with plastic wrap and chill in refrigerator for at least 2 hours. Before serving, cut into bite-sized pieces, taking care not to disturb topping. Serve on same platter. Makes about 40 pieces.

Rumaki

Chicken livers
Soy Sauce
Brown Sugar
Bacon
Water chestnuts, sliced

Marinate chicken livers 1–2 hours in soy sauce. Then roll each one in brown sugar and wrap with a piece of bacon, putting a slice of water chestnut inside the bacon. Secure with a toothpick. Broil, turning once, until liver is done—about 4–5 minutes on each side.

Popcorn makes a tasty appetizer when sprinkled with Parmesan cheese. It can also be sprinkled with nutritional yeast, which tastes much better than it sounds.

Franks Bourbon

To 1 pound of hot dogs cut into bite-sized pieces, add the following:

1 cup bourbon
2 onions, minced
½ cup brown sugar
1 tablespoon Worcestershire sauce
1 (12 or 14 ounce) bottle ketchup
1 (12 or 14 ounce) bottle chili sauce

Heat slowly, stirring occasionally, and simmer for 45 minutes. These should be refrigerated for at least 24 hours, and may be kept frozen for quite long periods.

To serve, reheat slowly to a boil. Serve with toothpicks from a hot tray or chafing dish.

Sausage Balls

1½ pound sausage meat—try mixing pork sausage with Italian mild sausage for a great flavor
1 cup water chestnuts, chopped

Mix and form into small balls, about the size of a walnut. Bake at 325 degrees for 30–35 minutes. Drain on paper towels and serve with toothpicks. Makes 36–40 balls, depending on size.

Meatball Crunchies

1 pound lean ground beef
½ pound lean ground pork
2 eggs slightly beaten
½ teaspoon salt
¼ cup fine dry breadcrumbs
1 tablespoon light soy sauce
¼ teaspoon garlic salt
1 (8 ounce) can water chestnuts, drained and chopped
For dipping: Teriyaki sauce, sweet and sour sauce, hot mustard sauce

Combine all meatball ingredients, mixing gently but thoroughly. Form into 1-inch balls. Arrange on the rack of a broiler pan and bake 15–18 minutes in a preheated 375-degree oven. Be sure they are well browned. Drain on paper towels, spear with toothpicks, and serve with assorted sauces for dipping. Makes 36–40 meatballs.

Sirloin Kabobs

⅓ cup light soy sauce
2 tablespoons maple syrup or 1 tablespoon brown sugar
¼ teaspoon ground ginger
1 clove garlic, crushed
1 teaspoon grated onion
¼ cup dry white wine
1 pound boneless top sirloin, partially frozen

In a bowl combine marinade ingredients and set aside. Cut meat into long thin slices, rather like bacon, and marinate in prepared mixture for an hour or more.

Lace meat strips on wooden kabob skewers, adding pieces of tomato or green pepper if you wish. Broil or cook on charcoal grill until done to your liking—it doesn't take long. Will serve 12–14 at cocktails.

Soups

Strafford, Vermont
Margaret Pembroke

Fiddlehead Fern Soup

This recipe comes from a native New Englander who hunts the early spring woods each year for the tiny, curled-up fiddleheads. These delicate little plantlets can be found all canned and ready to go in certain fancy food shops in Vermont these days, but the real joy is the search: early spring, the walk in the woods, the canoe trip down the river along whose banks the ferns grow.

Fiddleheads must be picked at just the right time—when the heads are just out of the ground and still tightly curled. Then the preparation: they must be cleaned of sand and last year's growth—the brown hulls that cling to the new green curlicues. It will take about four rinses in water to be sure they are ready for the cooking pot.

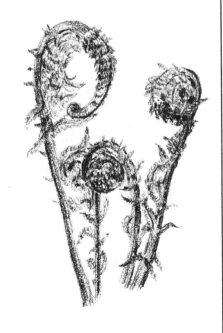

1 quart fiddlehead ferns
1½ quarts water
Evaporated milk
Skim milk
2 chicken bouillon cubes
Sherry, to taste
Salt and pepper, to taste

Boil ferns in water for 12 minutes. Drain and save broth. Whirl fiddleheads in blender with just enough broth to make a smooth purée.

In a saucepan combine equal amounts fern purée, fern broth, evaporated milk, skim milk. Add bouillon cubes and sherry to taste. Heat through but do not boil! Check seasonings, and add salt and pepper to taste. Serves 6–8.

Cheddar Cheese Soup from Shelburne Farms

3 tablespoons butter
1 cup chopped onions
1 cup chopped carrots
1 cup chopped celery
1 cup chopped green pepper
⅔ cup flour
3 cups chicken stock
3¼ cups milk
1 pound extra-sharp Vermont Cheddar cheese, shredded
1½ cups beer
½ cup heavy cream
Salt and pepper to taste

In a large, heavy saucepan, melt butter and sauté vegetables until they are crisp-tender. Sprinkle flour evenly over them and cook over medium heat, stirring, for 2–3 minutes, until flour loses raw taste. Slowly add chicken stock and continue to stir constantly until mixture is smooth.

In a separate pan, heat milk. Add shredded cheese, a little at a time, stirring until all is melted. Add to stock and vegetables. Continue to cook over medium heat, stirring, until soup begins to thicken. Add beer, cream, salt, and pepper to taste. Heat through, but do not allow to boil! Serves 10.

Shelburne Farms is a magnificent 1888 estate spreading for a thousand acres along Lake Champlain in Shelburne, near Burlington. Its large Queen Anne-style manor house and two massive barns with turrets and courtyards set along winding roads through forest and meadows, were built by one of Commodore Vanderbilt's granddaughters and her husband surprisingly far north of the accepted social latitudes of the time, which generally ended at Newport, R.I.

Best of all, everyone can enjoy it today, as descendants of the family still live there and have converted it to semi-public uses including agricultural programs, outdoor concerts and festivals, and the production of high-quality foodstuffs. Always a working farm, today Cheddar cheese made from its herd of Brown Swiss is sold widely and used in the kitchen of the manor house, now enjoying a renaissance as a luxurious country inn.

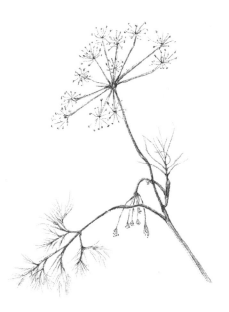

Tomato Bisque

1 pint (2 cups) tomatoes (if fresh, seeded and chopped; if canned, do not drain)
½ teaspoon baking soda
1 small onion studded with 5–6 cloves
2 teaspoons sugar
1 bay leaf
1 tablespoon dry parsley (or chopped fresh if you prefer)
2 cups milk
1 tablespoon butter or margarine
Salt and pepper, to taste

Heat tomatoes, which have been blended or processed until coarsely chopped. Add soda when they are hot to prevent curdling. Add the onion, sugar, bay leaf, and parsley. Simmer 5–10 minutes. Remove onion. Add milk, butter, salt and pepper. Flavor improves with reheating. Serves 2.

Carrot-Cider Soup

1 bunch carrots (8–10), roughly chopped
½ onion, roughly chopped
1 cooking apple, peeled, cored and chopped
¼ teaspoon ground cumin
½ cup apple cider
½ cup whole milk or light cream
Salt and pepper, to taste

Cook carrots and onions in water to cover until soft. Add apple and continue cooking until apple is tender. Transfer this mixture to blender or food processor and purée.

Return to saucepan. Add cumin, cider, milk, and seasonings to taste. Heat until hot but not boiling and add more cider if you want a thinner soup. Serves 4 .

Potato Leek Soup

As with most soups, exact quantities are not essential here—let your tastebuds do the fine tuning. However, be advised it's the dill that makes the difference!

5 tablespoons butter or margarine
2 or more leeks, washed and white parts chopped
2 or more carrots, sliced in thin rounds
6 cups chicken broth
2 teaspoons dried dill weed
2 teaspoons salt, or to taste
Black pepper, freshly ground (be generous)
1 bay leaf
6 potatoes, peeled and cubed
1 box (12 ounces) or 1 pound fresh mushrooms, sliced
1 cup half-and-half
¼ cup flour

Melt 3 tablespoons butter in large soup pot, and cook leeks and carrots until soft but not brown. Add broth, dill, salt, pepper, bay leaf, and potatoes. Simmer together about 20 minutes.

Meanwhile, sauté mushrooms in remaining butter and add to soup.

Mix half-and-half with flour and add. Cook, stirring, until soup thickens. Serves 8–10.

Winter in Vermont is long and cold. When it's chilly outside we need warmth inside. Simmering soups and stews are mainstays in the winter kitchen. But when summer finally comes we've learned to make our soups chilled and tucked full of fresh garden produce.

Mushroom-Spinach Soup

A "pantry shelf" lifesaver—easy, elegant, delicious.

1 (10 ounce) package frozen, chopped spinach
1 can cream of mushroom soup
1 can milk or light cream
Sherry, to taste

Cook spinach according to package directions. Drain well. Put the soup, undiluted, in the blender, add spinach and blend until spinach is the degree of fineness you desire.

Remove mixture to saucepan and add milk, increasing the amount if you want a thinner soup. Add sherry to taste. Heat to just below boiling point; serve. Serves 4.

Wild Rice Soup

½ cup wild rice, cooked according to package directions
2 cans cream of chicken soup
2 cans cream of mushroom soup
1 can chicken broth
1 soup can water
1 soup can dry white wine
1 grated onion
2 grated carrots
1 tablespoon Worcestershire sauce

Mix all ingredients together and heat through. Serves 12 generously.

This soup may be varied in a number of ways. Try adding bits of chicken or ham, sliced, sautéed mushrooms—let your imagination be your guide.

Walnut Soup

2 tablespoons butter
3 tablespoons flour
3 (10 ounce) cans chicken stock, or 4 cups homemade
½ teaspoon salt, or to taste
⅛ teaspoon pepper
1 bay leaf
¼ teaspoon curry powder
¾ cup chopped walnuts
1 cup cream (half-and-half or evaporated skim milk)

Melt butter in saucepan and combine with flour, cooking a few minutes and stirring constantly. Remove from heat and stir in stock; add seasonings, walnuts and cream. Return to heat and cook gently for twenty minutes and serve immediately. Or refrigerate for up to 4 hours and reheat. You may want to adjust seasonings. Serves 4–6.

Try passing a mug of soup at the end of drink time as a first course for dinner. This is also a good way to end a large cocktail party. Soup can be hot if weather is cold, or cold if weather is hot.

Peanut Soup from The Silent Kitchen

For 40	For 4
2 large onions, chopped	1 tablespoon
2–3 pounds carrots, chopped	1 tablespoon
4 tablespoons oil (peanut preferred)	1 tablespoon
10 quarts water	4 cups
1¼ cups brown rice	2 tablespoons
5 cups peanuts	½ cup
10 cups broccoli pieces, bite size	1 cup
5 cups mushrooms, sliced	½ cup
5 cans water chestnuts, sliced	½ can
¾ cup soy sauce	2 tablespoons
To taste instant bouillon powder	To taste

Brown onions and carrots in oil. Add water, rice, and peanuts and simmer 30 minutes. Add broccoli, mushrooms, and drained, sliced water chestnuts. Simmer until vegetables are almost tender, then add soy sauce. Cook till everything is tender and decide if you want to add bouillon.

The Silent Kitchen

Throughout this book there are recipes from The Silent Kitchen which include amounts suitable for a crowd. The Episcopal Diocese of Vermont has its headquarters and conference center at Rock Point, an oasis of quiet natural beauty on the shore of Lake Champlain at the edge of Burlington, Vermont's largest city. Each year during Advent and Lent silent retreats are held there among the pines along the rocky shores, and for several years a group of friends calling themselves "The Silent Kitchen" came together to provide food for these weekends. They worked in silence to produce memorable meals, and their recipes are a very special legacy to all of us.

Cream of Pumpkin Soup

A dramatic presentation of autumn bounty.

1 (10 pound) fresh pumpkin
1½ cups toasted croutons
1 cup grated Swiss cheese
3–4 cups light cream
Salt, to taste
Freshly ground pepper
Freshly ground nutmeg

Cut a circle from the top of the pumpkin, scrape it clean and cut the meat from it. Chop either by hand or in the food processor. Discard top. Scrape seeds and strings from inside the pumpkin, leaving flesh intact.

Fill shell with layers of croutons, chopped pumpkin, and cheese, alternating as often as your amounts will allow. Combine cream, salt, pepper, and nutmeg and pour into shell. Mixture should reach about ½ inch from the top.

Put pumpkin into baking pan (lined with foil) and bake for 2 hours at 325–350 degrees, stirring now and then, and scraping some of the meat from the sides of the pumpkin into the soup.

Served directly from the shell, the soup will be thick and hearty. For a more delicate dish, scrape additional meat from the pumpkin walls and purée entire mixture in the blender or processor. Return to shell for serving. Serves 6–8.

Pumpkin Soup

This soup was made by one of our committee members for a luncheon in honor of Joan Mondale at the festive 15th Anniversary of the Vermont Arts Council. The anticipated crisp November day went instead to 80 degrees. The soup was served chilled. Every bowl was scraped clean by four Vermont governors, legislators, senators, Arts Council Board members and the guest of honor. We thought of calling it 'Mondale Soup' or 'Governors' Soup.

7 tablespoons butter
6 scallions, chopped
1 onion, minced
3 cups pumpkin purée—fresh pumpkin only
6 cups chicken broth
½ teaspoon salt, or to taste
3 tablespoons flour
2 tablespoons butter
1 cup light cream
Croutons
Lightly salted whipped cream

Melt 4 tablespoons butter in large saucepan. Sauté scallions and onions until soft and golden. Add salt, pumpkin, and broth. Bring to boil, stirring. Simmer 10 minutes. Knead flour with butter; add gradually to soup, stirring with wire whisk. Bring soup to a boil, whisking until it thickens. Correct seasoning. Add cream and remaining tablespoon butter. Serve garnished with croutons and whipped cream. Serves 8.

Middlebury, Vt

Apple-Squash Soup

2–3 apples, chopped
1½ teaspoon lemon juice
¼ cup butter
1 onion, minced
3 pounds of butternut squash, peeled and cubed
1½ teaspoon dried thyme
4 cups chicken broth
¾ cup cider
½ cup bourbon
½ cup heavy cream

Mix chopped apples with lemon juice to prevent discoloration. In a large saucepan melt butter, add onion, and sauté until tender. Add apples, squash, thyme, and chicken broth. Bring to a boil and simmer, covered, 10 minutes, or until squash is tender. Cool 15 minutes.

Pour mixture through a strainer, reserving liquid. Purée solids. Combine liquids and purée in the saucepan. Add cider and bourbon. Heat through, then keep on low heat for one to two hours. At serving time, whisk in the cream. Serves 6–8.

Evaporated skim milk, which is found with other varieties of canned milk on your store shelves, can be substituted for cream in many recipes.

Winter Vegetable Soup

1 tablespoon bacon fat or margarine
1 medium onion, coarsely chopped
2 cups winter squash, peeled and cubed
2 cups turnip or rutabaga, peeled and cubed
4 cups beef broth or bouillon
½ teaspoon dried thyme
½ cup raw rice

In a 2-quart saucepan, sauté onion in fat. Add remaining ingredients and simmer until vegetables are very tender—about ½ hour.

Remove to blender or processor and purée. Return to saucepan, check and adjust seasonings, and thin to desired consistency with more broth or light cream, if you wish. Serve with a shake of nutmeg or a sprinkle of finely chopped parsley. Serves 4–5.

West Addison, Vt.

V-8 Soup from
The Silent Kitchen

For 40	*For 8*
5 cans V-8 Juice (46 ounce)	1 can
10 bouillon cubes	2
10 medium onions, chopped	2
10 green peppers, chopped	2
5 pounds carrots, grated	1 pound
5 cups water	1 cup
5 cans red kidney beans (15 ounce)	2 cans
1¼ cups rice or barley	2 tablespoons

Mix all ingredients together. Simmer about 1½ hours. Amounts and time are flexible. This soup freezes well, and is good and thick when reheated.

White Gazpacho

3 large cucumbers
3 cups chicken broth
1 pint sour cream
2 tablespoons vinegar
2 large cloves garlic
1½ teaspoons salt, or to taste
Minced parsley or minced red onion for garnish

The day before serving place in the blender the cucumbers and enough broth to allow a smooth blending. Add sour cream, vinegar, and garlic; blend thoroughly. You may do this in batches, combining all at the end. Then add remaining chicken broth and salt to taste. Allow to sit in the refrigerator overnight. Serve with garnish of your choice such as thin slices of radish. Serves 6.

Lentil Soup

1 (1 pound) bag lentils
6 cups water
1 large whole onion (studded with 3–4 cloves if you like)
1 zucchini, about 6 inches long, peeled and sliced
1 large potato, peeled and cubed
Olive oil
3 large cloves garlic, mashed
2 tablespoons dried mint
Juice of two lemons
Chicken stock to thin, if desired

In a large pot, combine lentils, water, and onion. Boil together until lentils are soft, about 45 minutes.

Remove to processor and blend until smooth. Return to cooking pot. Add zucchini and potato, and simmer together until vegetables are tender.

Meanwhile, sauté garlic and mint in a small amount of olive oil until garlic is light brown. Add to soup along with the lemon juice. If soup is thicker than you like, thin with stock or broth. Check the seasonings.

For more visual interest try sautéing sliced carrots with the garlic and mint—adds a nice, colorful touch. Serves 6.

Washday Soup

An old-time name for a hearty all-in-one meal that can be prepared before the activities of a busy day.

2 cups mixed dried beans—any kind
½ cup dried split peas
2 tablespoons each rice and barley
2 quarts cold water
2 large stalks celery, sliced
2 medium onions, sliced
2 medium potatoes, cubed
2 cups sliced or diced turnip
2 cups undrained canned tomatoes
Salt to taste
Pepper corns
Bay leaf
Ham bone or smoked hock

Soak beans, peas, rice and barley overnight in the 2 quarts water. Bring all to a boil, add vegetables and simmer 1 hour. Add ham bone and seasonings and simmer another hour or so. Add more water (or stock, if you prefer), and adjust seasonings. Serves 6–8.

For nonfat thickening of gravies and soup combine in a blender leftover potatoes, onions, and carrots.

Polish Cabbage Soup

Unusual and interesting, especially good reheated the next day.

1 head cabbage, shredded
1 large onion, chopped
3 tart apples, peeled and chopped (Granny Smith's are wonderful)
½ pound lamb, cut in chunks and including some bone
2 cups tomatoes
Juice of one lemon
⅓ cup sugar
1 teaspoon salt
Optional additions: red wine, caraway seeds

Cover shredded cabbage with lightly salted cold water and let stand about 10 minutes. Drain and dry—try rolling it up in kitchen towels.

Combine all ingredients with 2 quarts water, bring to a boil, and simmer 4 hours. Remove bones and taste for seasoning. Adjust and add optional extras if you want. Serves 6–8.

Cream of Vegetable Soup

This soup is delicious hot or cold.

1 tablespoon vegetable oil or margarine
½ cup chopped onion
1 clove garlic, minced
3 cups chicken broth
1 medium potato, peeled and chopped
3–4 cups of any of the following chopped:
    Broccoli
    Zucchini
    Spinach
    Swiss chard
1 (12 ounce) can evaporated skim milk
Salt and pepper to taste
Other herbs or spices of your choice: curry, thyme, dill, nutmeg, etc.

Sauté onion and garlic in oil until transluscent. Add broth and potato and simmer for 10 minutes. Add remaining vegetables and simmer until everything is tender. Purée in food processor until smooth. Return to pan; add milk and seasonings to your taste. Heat thoroughly—or chill—and serve. 4–6 servings.

If your cream soup (or cream sauce, for that matter) needs something but you can't tell just what, try adding some grated Parmesan cheese—a little if you just want to add body and enhanced flavor, a lot if you like a definite Parmesan taste.

Curried Zucchini Soup

From First Lady Barbara Bush

1 pound cleaned, unpeeled zucchini
2 tablespoons finely chopped onion or leek
1 clove garlic, minced
2 tablespoons butter or margarine
1 teaspoon curry powder, or to taste
¼ teaspoon salt
1¾ cups chicken broth
½ cup light cream

Chop unpeeled zucchini. In a heavy frying pan sauté with onions and garlic in the butter for 10–20 minutes. Stir occasionally, but do not let vegetables brown. Add curry powder and salt, stirring to mix. When vegetables are soft, put everything into a blender jar along with broth. Blend until smooth. Add cream, adjust seasoning, heat through, and serve. Makes 4 small servings. Can be served hot or cold, and is pretty with a parsley garnish.

June
Honeysuckle

Summer Garden Soup

Stir together:

1 (48 ounce) can tomato juice
1 tablespoon sugar
1 clove garlic, pressed
2 tablespoons lemon juice
1 teaspoon Worcestershire sauce
1½ teaspoons salt, or to taste

Add:

2 tomatoes, peeled, seeded and diced
2 carrots, finely diced
1 cup diced celery
¼ cup diced green pepper
1 small zucchini, halved and sliced

Chill overnight and serve garnished with croutons or fresh, minced herbs of your choice. Keeps in refrigerator for a week. Serves 6.

Gazpacho

2 large tomatoes, peeled and seeded
1 large sweet pepper, diced
1 clove garlic, minced
½ cup minced herbs: parsley, chives, basil, chervil, tarragon, etc., less if dried
½ cup olive oil
3 tablespoons lemon or lime juice
3 cups cold water or light chicken stock
1 mild onion, sliced thin
1 cucumber, peeled, seeded and diced
½ teaspoon paprika

Mix all ingredients together. Chill at least 4 hours and adjust seasoning to suit your taste. Serves 4.

Icy Lemon Soup

3 cans concentrated chicken broth
2 cups water
4 eggs
Juice of two lemons
Salt and white pepper, to taste

Heat chicken broth and water until mixture simmers. Beat eggs and lemon juice until well blended. Gradually beat one cup of hot soup mixture into eggs, combining well. Add remainder of soup very slowly (you don't want to scramble the eggs). Check to see if you would like more lemon juice, and add if you wish. Cool. Serve in your prettiest bowls or cups, garnished with thin slices of lemon or chopped parsley. Can be served either hot or cold. Serves 4–6.

If limiting sodium is important to you, start reading labels and avoid products that list it among the first 5 ingredients.

Cold Parsley Soup

4 tablespoons butter
1 large onion, chopped
2 stalks celery, chopped
2 large potatoes, peeled and cubed
3 (10 ounce) cans chicken stock or 1 quart homemade
Salt and pepper, to taste
1 cup fresh parsley, tightly packed and minced fine
½ cup cream

Melt butter in saucepan over low heat. Add onion and celery, cover pan, and "sweat" vegetables for 10 minutes. Stir now and then, and avoid browning.

Add potatoes, broth, salt, and pepper. Simmer for 15 minutes, or until potatoes are very tender. Set aside to cool.

When cool, purée mixture until very smooth. Return to saucepan and add parsley and cream. Reheat gently to blend flavors. Cool in refrigerator overnight. Serve cold garnished with thin slices of lemon.

Serves 6–8.

Combine leftover green salad with bouillon and tomato juice in a blender for a delicious gazpacho-like soup, hot or cold.

Eggs, Pasta, Rice, and Cheese

Cider Rice Pilaf

3 tablespoons butter
1 cup white or brown rice
Salt and pepper, to taste
½ cup chopped onion
¾ cup chopped celery
1 teaspoon grated orange peel
¼ cup minced parsley
¼ teaspoon dried rosemary or ¾ teaspoon fresh
1¾ cups apple cider

Melt butter in a skillet. Add rice and stir until golden. Add salt, pepper, onion, celery, and orange peel. Sauté 5 minutes more. Add half the parsley and all the rosemary.

In a separate pan bring the cider to a boil, then stir into rice. Cover the skillet and cook over low heat about ½ hour for white rice, or an hour for brown rice. Serve sprinkled with remaining parsley. Serves 4.

This is especially good with pork or lamb.

Zippy Pilaf

This becomes a main dish with the addition of leftover meat or chicken.

2 teaspoons oil
1 large onion, chopped
1 large clove garlic, minced
2 teaspoons powdered cumin
10 cherry tomatoes, quartered
½ teaspoon salt
¼ teaspoon cayenne pepper, or to taste
1 cup raw rice
1¾ cup chicken broth

Heat oil in saucepan over medium heat and sauté garlic, onions, and cumin for 2 minutes. Add tomatoes and cook 2 minutes more. Stir in salt, pepper, and rice. Add broth and bring to a boil. Cover tightly and simmer over very low heat 20 minutes. Rice is done when the liquid has evaporated. Serves 4.

"Timeless Rice" . . . an easy accompaniment to that oven dinner you've planned. For 4: in an oven-proof covered dish, sauté 1 cup rice in 1 or 2 tablespoons margarine, stirring until rice is lightly coated. Add 2 cups stock or broth, salt to taste, cover, and pop into your preheated oven. Rice will be done in about 45 minutes, but will hold indefinitely. When you are ready, just fluff with a fork and serve. Vary this basic recipe by adding chopped onions, mushrooms, leftover meat, etc., during cooking time, and/or chopped parsley just before serving.

Wild Rice Casserole

½ cup (1 stick) butter or margarine
2 small cans sliced mushrooms, or the equivalent fresh, sautéed
1 onion, chopped
2 tablespoons chopped green pepper
1 cup pecans, chopped
½ cup wild rice
½ cup white or brown rice
3 cups chicken broth
Salt and pepper, to taste

Sauté mushrooms, onion, and green pepper in butter. Add pecans and cook for one minute. Stir in rice.

Pour mixture into covered casserole, add broth and seasonings, cover and bake at 350 degrees for 1 hour. Serves 8.

Creamy Fettuccine with Vegetables

1 cup sliced carrots
1 cup sliced zucchini
1 cup broccoli flowerets
1 pound green beans, snipped and cut into 1-inch pieces
8 ounces fettuccine
1½ cups low-fat cottage cheese
⅓ cup skim milk
2 teaspoons dried basil
¼ cup chopped parsley
Parmesan cheese

Steam vegetables until tender. Cook pasta, drain, and set aside to cool.

Using a blender or food processor purée cottage cheese and milk; add basil and parsley. Taste for seasoning.

Combine vegetables and pasta. Pour sauce over all and top with Parmesan. Serve at room temperature or warmed a bit. Serves 6.

Even though there are no longer more cows than people in Vermont, dairy farming is still very important, and its products of milk, cream, yogurt and various cheeses come fresh to our kitchens.

Eggs, Pasta, Rice, and Cheese

Suzy's Tomato and Herb Pasta

3 tablespoons olive oil
2–3 cloves garlic, minced
1 medium onion, chopped
4 cups Italian plum tomatoes, coarsely chopped
3 tablespoons tomato paste
½ cup white wine
1 cup chopped parsley
½ teaspoon basil
½ teaspoon oregano
12–15 sliced black olives
Salt to taste
8 ounces fettuccine, cooked according to package directions

Sauté onion and garlic in oil. Add remaining ingredients and simmer over low heat for 20 minutes to 1 hour. Serve on hot fettuccine and pass grated Parmesan cheese. Serves 4.

Spaghetti with Fresh Tomato Sauce and Basil

4 ripe tomatoes, peeled, seeded and chopped (canned can be used if necessary)
1 pound mozzarella cheese, diced
¼ cup fresh basil, minced (about 20 leaves)
2 cloves garlic, crushed
5 tablespoons olive oil
½ teaspoon salt and pepper, to taste
1 pound spaghetti

Toss all ingredients except spaghetti together in a bowl and let stand for at least 30 minutes.

Cook and drain spaghetti. Pour tomato sauce over it and serve with grated Parmesan cheese. Serves 4.

Always store grated cheese in your freezer as it loses quality in just a few days in the refrigerator.

Golden Veggie Pasta

4 tablespoons margarine
2 tablespoons olive oil
2 medium onions, chopped
2 cloves garlic, chopped
1 tablespoon chopped fresh basil, or 1 teaspoon dried
1 tablespoon chopped fresh oregano, or 1 teaspoon dried
Salt and pepper, to taste
4 tomatoes, peeled and chopped
4 small zucchini, sliced
½ cup chicken broth—more if needed
1 pound small shell pasta
½ cup grated Parmesan cheese

Heat 2 tablespoons margarine and the oil. Add onion and garlic and sauté until onions are soft. Add basil, oregano, salt, pepper, tomatoes, zucchini, and broth. Simmer 5 minutes or until zucchini is just tender.

Boil the shells about 5 minutes—until not quite done—then drain and toss with veggie mixture. Spread in buttered baking dish and sprinkle with Parmesan cheese. Dot with 2 tablespoons margarine. Bake in a 350-degree oven for about 30 minutes, or until golden brown. Serves 4.

One pound of cheese equals 4 cups of loosely packed grated cheese.

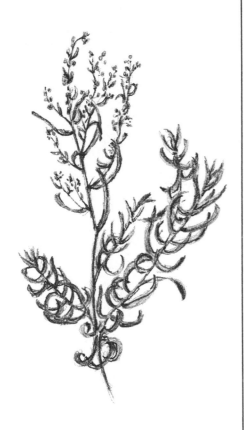

Pasta Veneziana

A cold sauce for hot pasta, and not for the fainthearted, but if you love garlic and olive oil, try this sensational recipe. The sauce is also wonderful on crackers the next day, should you have any left over.

3 (6 ounce) cans pitted ripe olives, chopped medium fine in food processor
2 tablespoons minced garlic
3 tablespoons grated Parmesan cheese
1 tablespoon grated Romano cheese
4 tablespoons finely chopped fresh parsley
1 teaspoon dried oregano
1 teaspoon dried basil
¼ teaspoon pepper
1½ cups olive oil
1 pound fettucine or linguine, cooked according to package directions
2–2½ cups halved cherry tomatoes

Mix all ingredients except pasta and tomatoes in a large bowl. Let stand for at least 1 hour before serving—longer is better.

At serving time whisk sauce well and toss with hot pasta. Add tomatoes and toss again. Serves 6. Makes 4 cups sauce, only part of which you may want to use with pasta—suit yourself.

Fettuccine with White Clam Sauce

2 dozen tiny littleneck clams (or 1 can chopped clams)
1 cup water
1 tablespoon chopped shallots or yellow onion
½ cup olive oil
Salt, to taste
1 teaspoon chopped garlic
2 tablespoons chopped parsley
¼ teaspoon red pepper flakes or dried hot red pepper
¼ cup white wine
1 tablespoon butter
2 tablespoons grated Parmesan cheese
8 ounces fettuccine

Wash and scrub the clams. Put them with the water in a covered saucepan over high heat and as they open up, shuck them and place in a small bowl. Pour any juices in saucepan over them and set aside.

Sauté shallots in the oil in a small saucepan over medium heat until translucent. Add garlic and sauté until lightly colored. Add parsley, hot pepper, and wine. Stir for a minute or so, salting to taste. (Sauce may be prepared to this point ahead of time.)

Remove clams from their juice and chop. Filter juice through a sieve lined with paper towels until there is ⅔ cup and add it to the wine mixture. Boil sauce until reduced by half. Add clams, turn them quickly in the hot sauce, and turn off heat. Add butter and cheese, mixing thoroughly.

Cook pasta. Drain and transfer to warm serving bowl and toss thoroughly with clam sauce. Serve immediately with additional cheese on the side if you wish. Serves 4.

Crab Spaghetti

½ pound thin spaghetti, broken into pieces and cooked
2 cups chopped onion
2 cloves garlic, crushed
½ pound mushrooms, chopped
½ pound Cheddar cheese, grated
½ cup sour cream
1½ teaspoons salt
½ teaspoon basil
½ cup stuffed green olives (optional)
3 (6 ounce) cans crabmeat

Cook spaghetti according to package directions and drain. Sauté onions, garlic, and mushrooms in a small amount of margarine.

Add remaining ingredients, mix well, and spread in a heat-proof casserole. Sprinkle top with crumbs, if you wish, and bake at 350 degrees for 1 hour. Serves 5–6.

When cooking with sour cream try these low-fat versions.

1. Purée 1 cup of low-fat cottage cheese with enough plain yogurt to make the right consistency.

2. Purée cottage cheese with 2 tablespoons of skim milk and 1 tablespoon of lemon juice.

Ham Linguine Florentine

Chopped fresh spinach makes a colorful, nutritious bed for this festive entrée.

½ cup sliced almonds
1½ cups sliced mushrooms
¾ cup chopped onion
3 tablespoons butter or margarine
3 tablespoons cooking oil
3 tablespoons flour
¾ teaspoon dried thyme
1 (13¾ ounce) can beef broth
¾ cup light cream or milk
¾ pound cooked ham, julienned
½ cup chopped parsley
3 tablespoons Dijon-style mustard
6 ounces linguine, cooked
8 ounces spinach, stemmed, coarsely chopped

In a heavy 12-inch skillet brown almonds over medium heat until golden; remove. In same skillet heat butter and oil and cook onions and mushrooms until onions are tender. Stir in flour and thyme and cook for 1–2 minutes. Take skillet off heat and stir in broth and cream, combining well. Return to heat and cook, stirring, 1–2 minutes more. Add half the almonds, the ham, parsley, and mustard. Mix in cooked linguine. Place spinach on serving platter or divide among dinner plates. Top with linguine mixture and sprinkle with remaining almonds. Serves 6.

Lavina's Spinach Lasagna

No tomatoes in this one—an interesting change from the expected. If you want a less pronounced spinach flavor use only 2 boxes of spinach.

If you lay out lasagna noodles on sheets of aluminum foil after they have been cooked, you will find them easier to handle when you assemble your recipe.

2 pounds low-fat cottage cheese
1 tablespoon chopped parsley
¼ cup (4 tablespoons) butter, melted
2 eggs, lightly beaten
Salt, pepper, garlic powder, to taste
1 pound Monterey Jack cheese, grated
9 lasagna noodles, cooked al dente and laid flat on aluminum foil
3 (2) packages frozen chopped spinach, cooked and drained
1 cup grated Parmesan cheese

Mix cottage cheese, parsley, butter, eggs, and seasonings.

Grease a 9- x 13-inch baking pan and layer in it as follows:

3 lasagna noodles
½ cottage cheese mixture
½ Monterey Jack
½ spinach
½ parmesan

Repeat, ending with noodles. Dot with more butter and sprinkle with a bit more Parmesan. Bake at 350 degrees for 35–40 minutes. Makes 12 servings.

Vegetarian Lasagna

Freeze any extra in individual servings, ready to microwave whenever you want a quick, healthy, delicious meal.

2 cups chopped onions (2 large)
2–4 cloves garlic, finely minced
½ pound fresh mushrooms, sliced
1 tablespoon oil or margarine
1 bunch broccoli, chopped (about 4 cups)
½ pound fresh spinach, washed, stemmed, and chopped (about 2 cups)
½ teaspoon any low-salt seasoning of your choice
2 cups low-fat cottage cheese
8 ounces part-skim mozzarella, shredded
Parmesan cheese
¼ cup chopped parsley
2 eggs
Salt and pepper, if desired
Oregano, basil, dill (dried) for sprinkling
3–5 cups ready-made spaghetti sauce
9 lasagna noodles, cooked al dente and spread on aluminum foil until needed

In a large skillet (electric fry-pan is perfect) sauté the onion, garlic, and mushrooms in the oil until they are soft. Add broccoli, spinach, and low-salt seasoning. Stir to combine, reduce heat, cover and simmer for about 5 minutes, or until broccoli is almost tender.

In a bowl, combine the cottage cheese, mozzarella, 3 tablespoons Parmesan, parsley, eggs, and salt and pepper if desired.

In a 9- x 13-inch baking dish spread ½–1 cup spaghetti sauce. Then layer the lasagna as follows:

3 lasagna noodles
½ egg-cheese mixture
½ vegetable mixture
spaghetti sauce to cover
generous sprinkling of oregano, basil, dill, Parmesan cheese

Avoid the step of boiling lasagna noodles by assembling your recipe with uncooked noodles, making sure you use about 32 ounces of sauce and then carefully pouring a cup of water around the edges of the assembled lasagna. Cover with foil, bake for 1 hour and 15 minutes, then let stand uncovered for 15 minutes (a vital step) before cutting and serving.

Repeat, ending with last three noodles covered with spaghetti sauce and sprinkled with more herbs and Parmesan. Bake, covered with foil, for about 30 minutes at 375 degrees. Remove foil and bake 5–10 minutes more until lasagna bubbles. Let stand 10 minutes before cutting. 12 servings.

Note: Preparation time can be simplified by using frozen broccoli and spinach, and canned mushrooms, but the result is not as good.

Spinach Soufflé

3 eggs
4–6 tablespoons flour
1 (10 ounce) package frozen chopped spinach, thawed and drained
2 cups low-fat cottage cheese
2 cups shredded sharp Cheddar cheese
1 teaspoon salt, if desired
Ground pepper, to taste

Preheat oven to 350 degrees. Beat eggs in a large bowl. Add flour and continue to beat until smooth. Add remaining ingredients and turn into a greased 2-quart casserole. Bake uncovered for an hour. Let stand 5–10 minutes before serving. Serves 4–6.

This recipe can be amended in a variety of ways: try adding sliced mushrooms, slivered ham, or chopped onion, for example. It may also be doubled or tripled if you have a huge crowd to feed—but watch the flour. You may use less flour than the mathematical amount for a softer finished texture. This is an easy, elegant dish, and a sure-fire crowd pleaser.

Many Vermont farm families made their own Cheddar cheese, and often supplied the local general store as well. Wedges would be cut from the big, yellow wheel on the counter. Today there are still cheese makers, now commercially making mozzarella, chevre, feta, and farmer cheese, as well as several styles of Cheddar.

Quick and Easy Quiche

The beauty here is that you don't have to fuss with pastry. It slices neatly, and could be enlivened by the addition of sautéed onions and peppers. A little nutmeg is also nice.

2 cups sliced vegetables (broccoli, asparagus, zucchini, etc.) cooked tender-crisp
1 cup shredded cheese—a mixture of Cheddar and Swiss is good
1 cup cottage cheese
3 eggs
1 cup milk
½ cup biscuit mix
Salt and pepper, to taste

Place vegetables in a greased 8-inch pie plate. Sprinkle with grated cheeses.

Mix cottage cheese, eggs, milk, seasonings, and biscuit mix in food processor (or blend thoroughly in some fashion) and pour over vegetables. Bake at 350 degrees for 30 minutes or so. Serves 4–6.

Eggs, Pasta, Rice, and Cheese

Easy Carrot Quiche

3 large potatoes, shredded
½ teaspoon salt
½ teaspoon pepper
2 tablespoons vegetable oil
2 cups shredded carrots
1 medium onion, chopped
1 clove garlic, minced
3 eggs
1 cup cottage cheese
½ cup shredded Swiss cheese
¾ cup milk
1 tablespoon parsley
3 tablespoons grated Parmesan cheese

High butterfat cheeses such as brie freeze well. Triple wrap in plastic, store in heavy plastic bag, and defrost slowly in the refrigerator.

Preheat oven to 425 degrees. Grease quiche pan or pie plate.

Mix grated potato with half the salt, pepper, and oil and spread on bottom of the greased dish. Bake 20 minutes or until lightly browned. Remove and reduce oven to 375 degrees.

Sauté carrots, onion, and garlic in remaining tablespoon oil over medium heat until softened.

Whisk together the eggs, cheeses, milk, parsley and remaining salt and pepper. Stir in carrot mixture and pour over potato crust. Sprinkle with Parmesan and bake for 30 minutes, or until lightly browned. Serves 6.

Fiesta Brunch Eggs

8 slices firm white or whole wheat bread
½ cup butter or margarine, softened
3 (8 ounce) packages grated Cheddar cheese
1 can green chilies, chopped
8 slices Canadian bacon, shredded
6 eggs
2½ cups milk
½ cup half-and-half
½ teaspoon salt
Cayenne, dry mustard, onion powder, to taste

Butter bread on both sides; cut into cubes. Butter a 9- x 13-inch casserole and spread bread cubes on bottom. Sprinkle with cheese, bacon, and chilies. Beat eggs with milk, half-and-half, and spices. Pour over all and refrigerate overnight.

Heat oven to 325 degrees and bake uncovered for 45 minutes. Serves 6–9.

Add a teaspoon of vinegar to the water when poaching an egg and it keeps the whites from spreading.

Zucchini-Sausage Pie

2 pounds zucchini, chopped
½ pound sausage, or more as desired
¼ cup onion, chopped
½ cup cracker crumbs
3 eggs, lightly beaten
⅛ teaspoon each thyme, garlic, rosemary
½ cup Parmesan cheese, grated

Cook zucchini 3 minutes and drain well. Sauté sausage and drain. Combine all ingredients. Place in pie pan or casserole dish and sprinkle with more cheese.

Bake 45 minutes at 350 degrees. Serves 4–6.

To separate eggs quickly and easily, break into a funnel over a glass or small bowl.

Sausage and Cheese Pie

Consider this for brunch or lunch.

1 pound Italian sausage, thinly sliced
2 eggs, beaten
1 (10 ounce) package chopped spinach, thawed and drained
8 ounces mozzarella cheese, grated
1 cup cottage cheese
½ cup milk
½ teaspoon salt
¼ teaspoon pepper
¼ teaspoon garlic
1 recipe pie crust dough

Cook sausage and drain. Combine eggs, spinach, cheese, cottage cheese, milk, garlic, salt, and pepper. Stir in sausage.

Line an 8- x 8-inch pan with half the pastry. Pour in sausage mixture. Cover with rest of pastry. Slit crust in several places and cover edges with foil. Bake 40 minutes at 350 degrees. Remove foil and bake 35 minutes longer. Let stand 10 minutes before cutting. Serves 4–6 as main course.

Poultry and Fish

Newbury, Vermont
M. Parlour

New England Chicken Pie

Chicken Pie was a favorite Sunday dinner on the farm, and remains a standard at church suppers to this day. It was easy to cook the chicken and make the gravy on Saturday. Then when you got home from church the next day, you could heat it up, top with baking powder biscuits, and pop it in the oven. In the old days we used fowl because it is more flavorful and less expensive, but chicken pieces from the supermarket work almost as well and take less time to cook.

Remember that traditional New England chicken pie contains no vegetables in the final dish. If you find a carrot or an onion in yours sometime, somewhere, know you are eating the Southern variation.

6 pounds chicken pieces
1 medium carrot
1 large onion
1 stalk celery plus some tops
1 bay leaf (a modern but tasty addition)
5 or 6 peppercorns

The day before: Cover chicken with water in a large pot and bring to a boil. Simmer 1–2 hours, or until chicken is tender and ready to slip off the bone. Do not boil! Remove chicken and let cool. Remove skin and bones, refrigerate chicken, and return skin and bones to the pot. Simmer another 2 hours. This step can be eliminated but adds more body to the gravy. Chill the broth and skim off fat, reserving some for the gravy.

To make the gravy: Make a roux of 4 tablespoons chicken fat and 4 tablespoons instant flour. Blend gently over low heat for about 3 minutes. Remove from heat. Stir in 4–5 cups chicken stock, and when blended and smooth return to heat and simmer, stirring, for a few minutes. Refrigerate if you are making it the day before.

To assemble and serve: Heat oven to 450 degrees. Lightly grease a large, shallow baking dish of a size that will hold the chicken in one layer. Arrange the chicken and cover with gravy. Set the dish in the hot oven while you make the biscuits. The gravy should be bubbling before you add biscuits to

Church and community suppers are numerous in summer and fall when everyone, tourists included, are invited to pull up a folding chair around a communal table. Chicken pie with a biscuit crust is the traditional main dish.

prevent them from being soggy. Make your favorite baking powder biscuit recipe and drop the dough in small lumps in the hot chicken mixture, or roll out dough and cut in rounds if you prefer. Bake in the hot oven until biscuits are golden brown. Serve immediately to 6–8 appreciative eaters.

Easy Roast Chicken

Elegant enough for special occasions, easy enough for everyday, this chicken lends itself to leftover magic.

1 roasting chicken
2 whole lemons
Margarine
Salt and pepper

Heat oven to 350 degrees. Wash and dry chicken. Wash lemons, pierce them deeply with a sharp fork and place in cavity of chicken. Rub skin with margarine and sprinkle with salt and pepper. Roast, covered, for about 1 hour. Then uncover and roast until bird is nicely browned, basting now and then. This will take approximately ½ hour. Bird is done when leg joint runs clear if pierced with a sharp knife.

A roasting chicken will weigh between 3½ and 5 pounds, and will serve approximately 4–6.

For a quick, low-fat main dish, heat several tablespoons light Italian salad dressing in a skillet, add some dried oregano, and stir over medium-to-high heat for 2 minutes. Sauté boned chicken breasts quickly in this mixture, sprinkling them toward the end with paprika and pepper. Serve with rice pilaf.

Easy Roast Chicken Leftovers

If you are lucky enough to have leftovers, try this. Reheat chicken and pour off the accumulated juices into a saucepan. They will have a wonderful lemon flavor. Remove meat from carcass, dice, and set aside. Mix some flour in a little chicken stock or water and add to pan juices, stirring until it thickens. Adjust amount and thickness here to suit yourself. Return diced chicken to the sauce, adding a bit of sautéed onion or sautéed sliced mushrooms if you like. Excellent on toast, rice, or patty shells.

Even if you have only bits of chicken left, don't throw a thing away. Scrape meat from bones, combine with lemony pan juices in food processor and purée. Add stock, evaporated skim milk, milk, half-and-half, or whatever suits you, and enjoy an unusual and delicious soup. Your imagination sets the only limits here.

Hopped-Up Chicken

4 chicken breasts, or any suitable combination of pieces
1 teaspoon salt
¼ teaspoon pepper
1 teaspoon each rosemary, marjoram, and oregano
¼ cup lemon juice
⅔ cup white wine or dry vermouth
2–3 tablespoons margarine or butter

Mix salt, pepper, and herbs and sprinkle liberally over chicken. Sauté in the butter or margarine until brown on all sides.

Add liquids to skillet, making sure they are well blended with pan juices. Cover and simmer until tender, gently basting and turning occasionally. The liquid will thicken and form a wonderful, piquant coating on the chicken pieces as it evaporates. Serves 4.

Chicken Breasts in Sherry-Mushroom Sauce

A low-fat, low-salt dish worthy of your most special occasions.

1 (10½ ounce) can no-salt chicken broth
2 tablespoons all-purpose flour
⅛ teaspoon salt (optional)
¼ teaspoon pepper
4 boneless, skinned chicken breast halves
Vegetable cooking spray
1 tablespoon margarine, melted
2 cups sliced fresh mushrooms
2 tablespoons minced shallots
¼ cup dry sherry or Madeira
1 tablespoon chopped fresh parsley

Place chicken broth in small saucepan. Bring to a boil over high heat and cook 5 minutes or until reduced to about 1 cup. Set aside.

Combine flour, salt, and pepper. Sprinkle over chicken. Coat a large skillet with cooking spray and place over medium to high heat until hot. Add chicken and cook until browned on all sides. Remove and set aside. Wipe skillet with paper towels.

Add mushrooms, margarine, and shallots to skillet, and cook over medium heat until mushrooms are lightly browned, stirring constantly. Add sherry and bring to a boil. Add broth and cook until sauce is reduced to 1¼ cups—about 7 minutes or so. Return chicken to skillet, reduce heat, cover and simmer about 10 minutes or until chicken is done.

Remove chicken to serving platter and keep warm. Cook sauce over high heat for 5 minutes, stir in parsley, and pour over chicken. Serves 4.

Try breading skinned chicken in rolled oats to add fiber and lower saturated fats.

Braised Chicken with Prunes

4 chicken breasts, split in half
1 onion, finely chopped
2 tablespoons oil
½ cup chicken broth
½ cup dry vermouth or white wine
2½ teaspoons curry powder, or to taste
½ teaspoon each ground ginger and cinnamon
1 cup pitted prunes
1 cup coarsely chopped carrots or red bell peppers—or mix them—or a cup of chopped fruit, such as apples, pears, or grapes
Salt, to taste

Brown chicken pieces and onions in the oil. Mix liquids and spices (try shaking them in a screw-top jar) and pour over chicken. Cover and simmer 15–20 minutes.

Add prunes, carrots, and/or peppers (or fruits), cover again, and simmer until chicken is tender and prunes are plump. Add water or broth if necessary.

Carefully remove chicken and vegetables (fruit) to serving dish. Reduce pan juices to a syrup and pour over chicken. Serve with rice or couscous. Serves 6–8.

Sesame Chicken
with Lemon Sauce

A lovely variation on that unbeatable lemon-chicken combination.

8 chicken breasts, skinned, boned, and halved
3–4 cups fresh bread crumbs
1 stick butter or margarine, melted
¾ cup sesame seeds

Dip chicken pieces in melted butter, then dredge in bread crumbs—chicken should be well covered. Place in shallow baking dish and sprinkle generously with sesame seeds. Drizzle any remaining butter over chicken. Dish may be prepared ahead and refrigerated at this point. Bake in a 350-degree oven for 45 minutes or until crumbs are golden brown.

Serve with lemon sauce:

3 tablespoons butter
3 tablespoons flour
1 cup milk
3 tablespoons lemon juice, or to taste
Salt and pepper to taste

Melt butter in saucepan, add flour, and whisk until thickened. Add milk and stir until thickened again. Add lemon juice—slowly so sauce doesn't curdle. Season and stir until it is the desired consistency. Serves 8.

Hot Chicken Salad

2 cups diced, cooked chicken or turkey
1½ cups chopped celery
2 tablespoons chopped scallions
½ teaspoon dried tarragon
1 tablespoon Worcestershire sauce
½ cup toasted, slivered almonds
2 tablespoons lemon juice
1 cup mayonnaise
Salt if desired

Preheat oven to 350 degrees. Mix all ingredients and place in a buttered 2-quart casserole.

Top with:

1 cup Chinese fried noodles (wide ones, if you can get them)
⅓ cup freshly grated Parmesan cheese

Bake 30 minutes, or until heated through. Serves 6.

Easy Chicken Casserole

You can keep the ingredients for this company-quality casserole in the freezer and on the shelf, and be ready for whatever happens!

4 whole chicken breasts, boned and split
Salt and pepper, to taste
6 slices Swiss cheese
1 can cream of chicken soup
½ cup white wine
2 cups seasoned stuffing mix
4 tablespoons butter, melted

Place chicken pieces in a shallow baking dish large enough to hold them in a single layer. Sprinkle with salt and pepper and top with cheese slices. Mix soup and wine until smooth and pour over all. Mix stuffing with melted butter and sprinkle evenly over top. Bake at 300 for 1½ hours. Serves 4–6.

Slim Jim Baked Chicken

4 chicken leg joints, skinned if you like
4 whole chicken breasts, also skinned if you like
1 teaspoon garlic salt
2 teaspoons paprika
½ teaspoon oregano
½ teaspoon freshly grated lemon peel
⅓ cup freshly squeezed lemon juice
½ cup water

Preheat oven to 400 degrees. Rub chicken pieces well with garlic salt and sprinkle with paprika. Place in shallow baking dish, "skin side" down, with larger pieces in the corners and smaller pieces in the center. Combine remaining ingredients and pour over chicken. Bake uncovered for 30 minutes. Turn pieces over and continue baking 30 minutes or more. Baste once or twice during baking. Serves 8.

Oven-Barbecued Chicken

3 pounds chicken pieces
Shortening for browning
2 medium onions, sliced
½ cup chopped celery
1 cup ketchup
1 cup water
¼ cup lemon juice
2 tablespoons brown sugar
2–3 tablespoons Worcestershire sauce
2 tablespoons vinegar

Heat oven to 325 degrees. Brown chicken in shortening. Place in a shallow baking pan.

Cook remaining ingredients slowly together, simmering for 10–15 minutes. Pour over chicken pieces and bake, uncovered, for 1½ hours. Serves 6.

Chicken or Turkey Creole

A tasty, colorful use for leftover turkey or chicken. Actually, the end result is good enough to warrant boiling up a chicken expressly for the purpose.

2½ cups fresh, sliced mushrooms (about 10–12 large)
½ cup coarsely chopped onion (1 medium)
¼ cup margarine
2 teaspoons fresh lemon juice (½ lemon)
1 cup coarsely chopped green pepper (1 medium)
½ cup sliced celery (1 or 2 stalks)
2 cups chopped tomatoes (3 medium)—canned, drained ones will do
2 tablespoons flour
1½ cups chicken stock
¼ cup white wine
2 cups cooked chicken or turkey, diced
1 teaspoon salt (optional)
⅛ teaspoon pepper

Sauté mushrooms and onions in margarine and lemon juice until onions are translucent and soft. Add remaining vegetables and cook until almost tender—about 5 minutes.

In a small bowl, combine flour and stock until mixture is smooth and add to vegetables. Add wine and cook until sauce begins to thicken, stirring now and then.

Add turkey or chicken and remaining seasonings. When heated through, serve on patty shells or rice. May be refrigerated and reheated. Serves 6.

You can use cornstarch or arrowroot as a thickener instead of roux, which contains butter.

Chicken-Shrimp Gumbo

1 (5 pound) stewing chicken, cut up
1 teaspoon salt
½ cup shortening
½ cup flour
1 cup chopped onion
1 clove garlic, crushed
2 tablespoons Worcestershire sauce
1 tablespoon lemon juice
½ teaspoon black pepper
½ teaspoon powdered thyme
2 pounds uncooked, deveined shrimp
½ cup chopped celery
½ cup chopped green onion
½ cup chopped parsley

Sprinkle chicken pieces with salt. Melt shortening in large pot. Add chicken and brown on all sides. Remove and set aside.

Stir flour into hot fat in which chicken was browned. Stir over low heat until flour is golden brown. Add onion and garlic. Stir until they are transparent.

Stir in 2 cups water. Add chicken, Worcestershire, lemon juice, pepper, and thyme. Cook, covered, over low heat for 1½ hours or until chicken is tender.

Stir in shrimp, celery, and green onion. Simmer 30 minutes. Remove chicken and shrimp to serving platter. Boil remaining liquid, stirring constantly, until thick and smooth. Pour over chicken and decorate with parsley. Serve with rice. Serves 6 8.

Portuguese Chicken with Bacon

12 chicken legs
24 slices bacon, cut into small pieces
½ teaspoon (more or less) salt
¼ teaspoon (more or less) dried oregano
2 cups beer

Heat oven to 325 degrees. Put chicken legs in a heavy, shallow baking dish and sprinkle with bacon pieces. Mix salt and oregano together and sprinkle over meat. Pour in the beer so as not to disturb the bacon and seasonings and bake, covered, for ¾ hour or so. Check at the half-hour mark and test doneness by piercing with a fork.

Good with rice or noodles. Serves 6 if legs, 12 if whole joints.

The flavor of spices will intensify if, before adding to the recipe, you roast them on top of the stove in a heavy skillet.

Hungarian Chicken Paprikas

1 onion, chopped
3 tablespoons shortening
1 tablespoon paprika—sweet Hungarian, if possible
4–5 pounds chicken pieces
1 tablespoon salt, or to taste
¼ teaspoon black pepper
1½ cups tomato juice
1 pint sour cream

Brown onion in shortening. Add paprika, chicken, salt, and pepper. Continue cooking for 20 minutes, browning chicken on all sides. Add tomato juice, cover, and simmer until tender. Remove chicken. Add sour cream to pan juices and mix well. Heat through, but do not allow to boil. Combine chicken with sauce and serve with rice or noodles. Serves 8.

East Indian Chicken

Heart healthy, easy, eminently reheatable.

8–10 pieces chicken, skinned
2 tablespoons olive oil
2 medium onions, thinly sliced
2–3 cloves garlic, minced
1 teaspoon ginger
1–3 tablespoons curry powder
1 tablespoon chili powder
1 cup chicken stock
1 fresh tomato, coarsely chopped
1 cup low-fat cottage cheese, sieved or smoothed in the blender
Dash of salt, if necessary

In a large skillet or Dutch oven, lightly brown chicken pieces in the oil. Add onions, garlic, ginger, curry powder, chili powder, and ½ cup of the chicken stock. Simmer, covered, for 20 minutes.

Add tomato, remaining chicken stock, cottage cheese and salt. Simmer another 20 minutes. Serve with rice and Indian "boys": peanuts, chutney, sliced banana, raisins, minced scallions, shredded coconut, etc. Serves 6.

Chicken Vindaloo

A spicy dish—be sure to include some "coolers" (raisins, coconut, chopped bananas) along with the chutney and peanuts. A good make-ahead dish.

4–5 pounds chicken—either whole pieces, or boned and
    cut into bite-sized pieces.
1 teaspoon salt (optional)
¼ teaspoon cayenne pepper
2 teaspoons lemon juice
2 dried, red chilies
4 cloves garlic
1 (1½-inch) piece fresh ginger, peeled and chopped
¾ teaspoon ground cumin, or 1 teaspoon cumin seeds
1½ teaspoon ground coriander, or 2 teaspoons seeds
1 teaspoon black peppercorns
1 cinnamon stick
4 cloves
2 tablespoons malt vinegar
2 tablespoons oil
2 medium onions, chopped
1 teaspoon turmeric
2½ cups chicken broth

Sprinkle chicken pieces with salt, pepper, and lemon juice. Set aside for 30 minutes.

Put spices and vinegar in the blender and purée, adding more vinegar if needed.

Heat 2 tablespoons oil in a pan. When hot, add onions and fry, stirring, until they are golden brown. Stir in turmeric and spice purée and fry for 5 minutes, stirring constantly. Add a spoonful or 2 of water if the mixture becomes too dry. Add chicken and fry until evenly browned. Pour in broth; bring to a boil. Cover pan, reduce heat to low, and simmer 45 minutes or until chicken is cooked through.

If you wish to thicken the sauce, mix about 3 tablespoons cornstarch with ½ cup cold water and stir into chicken. Serve over rice. Serves 6–8.

Get to know your local health food store or food co-op. If your town is anything like Burlington, these will be your best sources of herbs and spices, especially those expensive and infrequently used ones that may make a recipe seem too exotic to be worth trying. You will be able to spoon out as much or as little as you need, save clutter on your spice shelf, and be assured of fresh, flavorful seasonings.

Hao Yu Pao Chi

(Chicken in Casserole, Cantonese Style)

6 dried Chinese black mushrooms
1 (3 pound) chicken, or equivalent amount pieces
1 teaspoon salt
1 teaspoon sugar
2 tablespoons cornstarch
3 tablespoons light soy sauce
1 tablespoon dark soy sauce
2 tablespoons oyster sauce
1 teaspoon sesame oil

Wash and soak the mushrooms in ½ cup warm water for 30 minutes. Remove and discard stems and cut each mushroom in half. Set aside.

Clean and wash chicken in water. Place in large mixing bowl. Combine marinade ingredients and add along with cut-up mushrooms to the chicken pieces. Toss well and let stand for 30 minutes or more.

3 tablespoons peanut or corn oil
4 cloves garlic, crushed
1 scallion, cut into 1-inch pieces
4 thin slices ginger root

On the stove heat a heatproof casserole or heavy pot until hot and add the oil. Stir in garlic, scallion, and ginger. Stir-fry for 1 minute. Add chicken and marinade. Stir-fry for 2 minutes. Cover and let cook over medium-low heat for about 30 minutes or until chicken pieces are tender. Stir often during cooking to prevent sticking. Juice will form—don't add water. Serve with rice. Serves 6.

Oriental Chicken Legs

Fantastic flavor.

Chopped peel of one orange
1 cup orange juice
½ cup soy sauce
Red pepper flakes
½ cup honey
1 cup chicken broth
½ teaspoon ground ginger
½ teaspoon Five Spice Chinese seasoning, if you have it, *or*
    ½–1 teaspoon Chinese mustard
12 chicken legs

Mix liquids and seasonings in the blender and purée. Arrange legs in a baking dish and pour blended mixture over them. Marinate for several hours.

Heat oven to 350 degrees and bake for 1 hour or until chicken is tender and very brown.

Remove legs to serving dish and skim fat from sauce, which can be thickened, if you like, with 2 tablespoons cornstarch. Heat, stirring, and pour over chicken. Serves 6.

Turkey Breast Chinoise

A festive centerpiece for a buffet table, goes well with everything, and is the inspired invention of a committee member.

1 (4–6 pound) turkey breast, rinsed and dried
3 cloves garlic, mashed
1 teaspoon salt
1–2 tablespoons butter or margarine

Mix garlic, salt, and butter together and rub well over the turkey breast. Force mixture under the skin where possible. Then combine in the blender:

½ cup lemon juice
½ cup olive oil
1 tablespoon molasses
1–1½ inch ginger root, peeled and sliced
¼ cup soy sauce

Whirl in the blender until ginger is puréed—and this takes longer than you expect, so don't despair.

Place breast in a deep bowl or a plastic bag and pour marinade over it. Seal well, and marinate for at least 6 hours—overnight is even better. Turn breast occasionally.

Several hours before you plan to serve, heat oven to 350 degrees. Put turkey into a roasting pan, pour marinade over it and roast for 1½ to 2 hours, or until a meat thermometer registers "done." Let stand 20 minutes before slicing.

"Vermont Turkey" means the best of the birds. Why? Because cold nights encourage an extra layer of fat for natural basting, the turkeys are sold very fresh, and are fully mature at holiday time. Since no Vermont turkeys can be sold out of state because the state has no federal turkey inspection, those mentioned on menus beyond the borders are impostors.

Turkey Breast Mediterranean

Another variation on the marinated turkey breast theme. Unusual and delicious; best served with pasta or rice.

1 (4–6 pound) turkey breast
2 teaspoons salt
½ teaspoon pepper
2 cloves garlic, crushed
1 tablespoon butter or margarine

Make a paste of the salt, pepper, garlic, and margarine and rub well over washed, dried turkey breast.

Combine in a bowl:

½ cup olive oil
½ cup white wine vinegar
2 medium tomatoes, peeled, seeded and chopped
2 medium green peppers, peeled, seeded and chopped
½ cup chopped parsley
1 (2¼ ounce) can pitted ripe olives, drained and sliced

Place breast in the marinade either in a heavy plastic bag or in a deep bowl, seal well, and refrigerate overnight, turning occasionally.

When ready to cook, heat oven to 350 degrees. Put turkey in a roasting pan, pour marinade over it, letting vegetables settle to the bottom, and roast for 2–2½ hours. Let stand before slicing. Serves 10–12.

For a sauce, degrease pan juices and vegetables, and serve along with the turkey.

Pheasant

3 pheasants, split
¼ cup butter
2 cups sliced mushrooms
2 tablespoons lemon juice
1 cup dry white wine
½ cup chopped onion
1 teaspoon salt
Fresh ground pepper

Sauté pheasant halves in butter until golden—about 10 minutes. Remove and add onion and mushrooms. Sauté a few minutes, stirring. Return pheasant to pan and add remaining ingredients. Simmer until birds are tender.

Remove birds to warm serving platter and thicken pan juices with a bit of flour. Pour over pheasant. Serve with wild rice. Serves 6.

Bluefish with Pesto and Tomato

Bluefish is a particular favorite in New England. A dark fish with a fairly pronounced flavor, it can be replaced with something similar, if you prefer.

2 pounds bluefish fillets, or equivalent amount of another fish
Olive oil
Salt and pepper
Juice of half a lemon
½ cup pesto
Tomatoes, thinly sliced

Preheat broiler. Line broiler pan with aluminum foil and brush with olive oil. Lay fish fillets in pan, brush with more olive oil and sprinkle with salt and pepper, if desired. Dribble lemon juice over them. Broil 2 inches away from heat, allowing 10 minutes for each measured inch of thickness. Baste with olive oil once, and *don't* turn over. When they are flaky, they are done.

Remove to serving plate(s) and on each fillet, spoon a line of pesto (see page 266) down the middle and top with thin slices of tomato. Serves 4.

Ice fishing shanties
Chimney Point, Vt.
Lake Champlain

Lake Perch

These fish, a favorite in Vermont, are best in winter when they are sweet and firm, freshly caught from a frozen lake.

1½ pounds lake perch
½ cup milk
¾ cup flour
Salt and pepper

Other seasonings of your choice: oregano, basil, parsley, etc.

Dip fillets in milk, then in seasoned flour. Cornmeal can be added to flour for more crunch. Fry fillets in enough butter or margarine to bubble up around fish. Turn once. These tiny fish are done when they are golden brown, about 5–7 minutes. Serves 3–4.

Scallop Sauté

1 pound bay scallops, rinsed and dried on paper towels
½ pound mushrooms, washed and sliced
2 coins candied ginger, slivered
2 tablespoons vegetable oil or margarine
1 teaspoon soy sauce
Salt and pepper, to taste
1 lemon

Sauté scallops, mushrooms, and ginger in the oil or margarine for 6–8 minutes. Remove to a warm serving dish.

Reduce liquid remaining in the sauté pan and season with soy sauce, salt, pepper, and juice of ¼ lemon. Adjust seasonings to your taste and pour sauce over scallop-mushroom mixture. Serve with lemon wedges. Serves 3–4.

Small, sweet lake perch and tiny, silvery smelt are best in winter, caught by ice fishermen in the cold, northern lakes. They are sold in some fish markets and food stores in northern Vermont but very rarely served in restaurants. This is a local specialty you have to enjoy at home.

Stuffed Sole

2 tablespoons butter
½ teaspoon seasoned salt
3 teaspoons lemon juice
¼ teaspoon white horseradish
5 drops tabasco sauce
⅓ cup heavy cream
1 can crabmeat or 1 (6 ounce) package frozen crab
4 fillets of sole
2 tablespoons melted butter
Chopped parsley

Melt 2 tablespoons butter, add salt, and 1 teaspoon lemon juice, horseradish, and tabasco. Blend in cream and cook, stirring constantly, until it comes to a boil—but do not let it boil! Remove from heat and add crabmeat.

Grease a shallow casserole and place 2 fillets on bottom. Pour crab mixture on top, cover with remaining sole. Spoon melted butter and remaining 2 teaspoons lemon juice over all. Sprinkle with parsley and bake at 350 degrees for 30 minutes. Serves 2.

Sole with Pine Nuts

This recipe also works well with sea bass, red snapper, or flounder.

½ cup shelled pine nuts
4 skinless fish fillets of your choice (about 1½ pounds)
Salt and freshly ground pepper to taste
2 tablespoons vegetable oil
2 tablespoons unsalted butter
¼ cup drained capers
1 tablespoon fresh lemon juice
2 tablespoons finely chopped parsley

Grind pine nuts in a food processor or chop extremely fine. Season fish with salt and pepper, then dredge well in nuts on both sides.

Heat oil over medium heat in a large (preferably nonstick) skillet. Sauté fish until golden brown on one side—about 3 minutes. Turn and cook 2 minutes more. Adjust times here according to thickness of your fish, and when they are done (test by flaking with a fork), transfer to warm plates.

In a clean skillet, heat butter over high heat. When it begins to turn brown, add capers. Shake skillet and stir for about a minute. Add lemon juice. Pour mixture over fillets. Garnish with parsley. Serves 4.

Baked Swordfish Steaks

6 swordfish steaks, at least 4 ounces each, ¾–1 inch thick (or use tuna if you prefer)
3 tablespoons olive or vegetable oil
2 tablespoons lemon juice
1 tablespoon white port or sherry
1 tablespoon water
1 tablespoon light soy sauce
3 cloves garlic, minced
¼ teaspoon ground ginger or 1 tablespoon minced fresh ginger
1+ teaspoon grated lemon rind
¼ teaspoon ground black pepper

Lay fish steaks in a shallow glass baking dish just large enough to hold them in one layer. Combine remaining ingredients and pour over the fish, brushing to coat well. Cover and refrigerate four hours or more.

Preheat oven to 450 degrees. Pour off most of the marinade (save it) and bake fish for about 15 minutes.

Or

Grill in a hot skillet for 3 minutes on each side until springy-firm.

Or

Microwave!

Pour reserved marinade in blender and whirl until smooth. Place in saucepan, adjust seasonings, heat, and serve with cooked fish. Serves 6.

Poultry and Fish

Fish à la Microwave

Fish cooked in the microwave is quick and easy, of course. It also remains very moist and tender. Cod, haddock, scrod, and salmon can all be cooked as suggested here.

Arrange 2 pounds of fish fillets in an 8- or 9-inch glass baking dish with thick edges of fish toward the outside of the dish. Cover with grated cheese, butter, onion flakes, lemon juice, salt, and other seasonings of your choice.

Cover pan with waxed paper and microwave for 11–13 minutes on high. Drain liquid and let stand, covered, for 5 minutes to complete cooking. Test for doneness by flaking with a fork.

Because microwave ovens vary, these instructions are guidelines only—this recipe was devised for a 500-watt oven, and serves 4.

Additional note: 1 pound of fish will require 9–10 minutes on high.

Baked Scallops à la Microwave

1 pound sea or bay scallops, rinsed
2 tablespoons lemon juice
1 tablespoon Italian-seasoned bread crumbs
Nonfat vegetable spray or 2 tablespoons margarine

Place scallops in a microwave baking dish in 1 layer. Sprinkle with lemon juice and bread crumbs. Spray with vegetable spray or dot with margarine. Cover with plastic wrap and microwave for 6 minutes at 75% power. Turn fish halfway through cooking time and serve immediately. Serves 3–4.

Fish Fillets with Mushrooms and White Wine Sauce

2 (10 ounce) packages frozen chopped spinach
2 (10 ounce) packages frozen chopped broccoli
3 pounds fish fillets (bass, cod, scrod, etc.)
Lemon pepper marinade (found on the supermarket spice shelf)
5–6 tablespoons butter or margarine
¼–⅓ cup flour
10 ounces milk or one can cream of mushroom soup (use ¼ cup flour with
    soup, ⅓ cup with milk.)
½ cup dry sherry
¼ pound fresh mushroooms, sliced and sauteed
Salt, pepper, cayenne
Grated Parmesan cheese
Sliced almonds

Cook and thoroughly drain spinach and broccoli. Mix and spread in a buttered, shallow baking dish.

Place fish in another shallow baking pan, sprinkle with lemon pepper marinade and dot with 3–4 tablespoons butter. Bake at 350 degrees for about 7 minutes, or until fish is not quite done. Pour juices into a heavy saucepan and place fish on top of vegetables.

Reduce fish stock and add remaining butter. Stir in flour and cook until smooth and faintly colored. Remove from heat and add milk, stirring constantly until blended and smooth. Return to heat, add sherry and bring to the simmer. Cook until you have a thick, white sauce. Add sautéed mushrooms and seasonings to taste. Pour over fish and sprinkle with cheese and almonds. Bake at 400 degrees about 15–20 minutes until bubbly and lightly browned. May be frozen, except for the almonds, and reheated accordingly. Serves 8.

Shrimp or Scallops Provençal

2 pounds shrimp or 1½ pounds scallops
2 pounds ripe tomatoes—or equivalent amount of canned, drained
4 tablespoons olive oil
Freshly ground pepper
4 tablespoons butter or margarine
1 tablespoon fresh garlic, pressed (3–4 cloves)
2 tablespoons fresh basil or 1 tablespoon dried
1 tablespoon minced parsley

Shell and devein shrimp and set aside. Peel and core tomatoes. Cut in half crosswise and squeeze to remove seeds. Cut into ½-inch pieces.

Heat 3 tablespoons olive oil in skillet and add tomatoes, salt, and pepper. Cook about 5 minutes or until most of tomato liquid evaporates.

In another skillet heat remaining oil with butter or margarine and sauté seafood 3–4 minutes until just cooked through. Add garlic and toss to blend. Do not overcook!

Pour tomatoes over cooked pasta or rice, top with seafood and sprinkle with basil and parsley. Serves 4.

Baked Stuffed Shrimp

This dish can be made early in the day, refrigerated, and baked just before serving.

12 large, jumbo shrimp in their shells
½ pound scallops
8 tablespoons (1 stick) butter or margarine, melted
½ teaspoon paprika
4 tablespoons crushed potato chips
½ cup cracker crumbs
6 tablespoons grated Parmesan cheese
3–4 tablespoons sherry

Cut raw, unshelled shrimp down the abdomen and remove the vein. With shrimp still in their shells, open them out, flattening each one and "butterflying" it with a toothpick through each end. Place them in a greased baking dish large enough to hold them in a single layer.

Chop scallops and divide among the shrimp.

Melt butter and add remaining ingredients. Place this stuffing mixture over the scallops and shrimp. Bake uncovered at 350 degrees for 35 minutes. Serves 4.

June
Honeysuckle

Poultry and Fish

Baked Fish Creole

Easy to cook, easy on the calories, easy to clean up.

1½ pounds haddock fillets
Salt and pepper
1 medium onion, chopped
1 small green pepper, chopped
¼ cup chopped celery
1 pint-sized can stewed tomatoes, drained
3 tablespoons buttered bread or cracker crumbs

Heat oven to 400 degrees. Line baking pan with foil and grease it.

Place fillets on foil and season them to taste. Sprinkle chopped vegetables evenly over them. Then add drained tomatoes. Cover with buttered crumbs. Bake until fish flakes—about 25 minutes. Don't overcook. Serves 5–6.

Baked Fish with Cheese Dressing

1½ pounds haddock
1 medium onion, sliced
2 tablespoons margarine
½ cup soft bread crumbs (about 3 slices bread)
1 cup grated Cheddar cheese
¾ cup milk
¼ teaspoon each salt, pepper, paprika

Heat oven to 400 degrees. Put fish in greased pan. Sauté thin slices of onion in margarine until tender but not brown. Add bread crumbs, cheese, salt, pepper, and paprika. Spread this dressing over fish. Pour milk around fish and bake for 20–30 minutes, or until fish flakes, uncovered. Serves 4–5.

Shrimp Casserole

6½ tablespoons butter or margarine
4½ tablespoons flour
¾ cup milk
¾ cup cream
1 tablespoon Worcestershire sauce
¼ cup dry sherry
¼ pound fresh mushrooms, sliced
1 can artichoke hearts, drained and halved
1 pound large, cooked shrimp
¼ cup grated Parmesan cheese

Make a cream sauce with 4½ tablespoons butter, flour, milk, and cream. Add salt and pepper to taste along with Worcestershire sauce and sherry. Stir until smooth.

Use remaining butter to sauté sliced mushrooms until they are golden brown and have given up their juices.

In a greased baking dish, place the artichoke hearts, the shrimp and the sautéed mushrooms. Pour the white sauce over all and sprinkle with Parmesan cheese. You may also want a sprinkle of paprika for color. Bake at 325 degrees for 20–25 minutes. Serves 4–6.

Lobster shells can be put to good use making Lobster Butter. This flavored butter goes well with any fish or shellfish and freezes well. Dry 1 lobster shell in oven until brittle, pulverize in a mortar or processor, then place in a double boiler with at least ¼ pound butter and 2 tablespoons water. Heat for 20 minutes before straining, pouring a little boiling water over shells to remove butter. Refrigerate to harden.

Crabmeat Casserole

8–10 slices white bread, cubed (depends on thickness of bread)
1 cup finely chopped celery
1 tablespoon margarine
1 pound crabmeat
1 medium onion, chopped
½ cup chopped green peppers
½ cup mayonnaise
4 eggs
2 cups milk
1 cup grated Cheddar cheese

Cook celery in margarine for 10 minutes; drain. Mix it with crabmeat, onion, peppers, and mayonnaise.

In a greased 2½-quart casserole, spread ½ the bread cubes evenly on the bottom. Cover with crabmeat mixture, then with remaining bread cubes.

Beat eggs with milk and pour over all. Cover and refrigerate overnight. Before baking, sprinkle cheese over the top. Bake uncovered at 250 degrees for 1½ hours. Serves 6–8. Chicken or ham could be used instead of crabmeat.

Quick Crab Cakes

1 pound fresh crabmeat
½ cup seasoned dry breadcrumbs
1 egg, beaten to blend
2 tablespoons mayonnaise
2 tablespoons whipping cream (absolutely essential)
2 tablespoons minced green onion
1 tablespoon chopped fresh parsley
1 teaspoon Worcestershire sauce
1 teaspoon Dijon-style mustard
A few drops hot pepper sauce
Salt and freshly ground pepper

Mix all ingredients together and form into 8 cakes. Dredge lightly in a mixture of ⅔ cup flour and ½ teaspoon paprika. Sauté until golden in vegetable oil. Serves 4.

Marinade for Swordfish

½ cup lemon juice
2 tablespoons olive oil
1 teaspoon salt
Pepper
½ clove garlic, mashed
½ teaspoon dried oregano

Combine all ingredients. Pour over swordfish and let stand for several hours. Bake or broil until fish flakes.

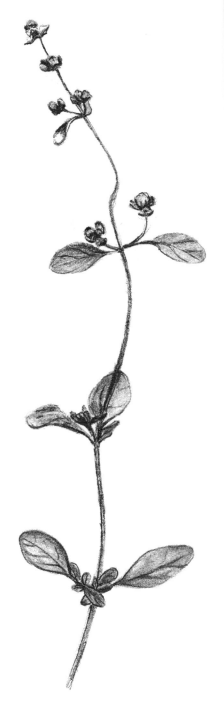

Seafood Lasagna

This dish was created for seafood, and is an especially good choice for a festive buffet. But it also works with cooked turkey or chicken—a great addition to your basic repertoire of reliable recipes.

1 pound lasagna noodles
¾ pound peeled, deveined shrimp
¾ pound scallops
2 cups white wine
2 cups stock (fish or chicken depending on what you're making)
6 tablespoons butter
½ cup flour
Salt, pepper
Paprika
Sherry, to taste
2 pounds sharp Cheddar cheese, grated

Cook lasagna noodles al dente according to package directions and cool on sheets of aluminum foil.

In a large saucepan, cook seafood in wine and stock for 3–5 minutes. Save the stock for the sauce. Remove seafood to food processor and chop coarsely. In saucepan, melt butter, add flour and seasonings, and cook, stirring, for a few minutes. Stir in 2 cups of the wine-stock mixture and cook until thickened. Add seafood mixture and set aside.

Layer noodles, cheese and seafood mixture, in that order, in a greased lasagna pan, finishing with a layer of cheese. Bake at 375 degrees for 45 minutes, or until bubbly. Let stand 10 minutes before serving. Serves 10–12 and freezes well.

Meats

Northeast Kingdom Lamb

5 tablespoons unsalted butter
2 or more pounds lamb from the leg, cut in 1-inch cubes
¼ pound pork, cut into smaller cubes
2 cups onion, chopped
2 tablespoons sugar
1½ cups beef stock or broth
2 teaspoons salt
½ teaspoon fresh ground pepper
2½ dozen dried apricot halves
2 cups pumpkin or butternut squash, peeled and cubed
2 cups green beans in ½-inch pieces
1 (20 ounce) can white kidney beans (cannellini), drained
¼ cup walnuts, coarsely chopped
2 tablespoons fresh dill, chopped (optional)

In a heavy casserole with a tight lid let butter begin to bubble over medium-high heat. Brown lamb in several batches. With slotted spoon remove lamb to another dish and brown the pork. Remove it also to the other dish.

Add onions to the casserole and cook until they are limp but not brown, about 3 minutes. Add sugar and let it caramelize for a few minutes on the bottom of the casserole. Add stock, salt, and pepper, and bring to a simmer. Add meats and simmer covered for about half an hour. At this point it may be left for several hours or overnight.

To complete, add apricots and pumpkin to the casserole, simmer and cook gently, covered, for 10 minutes. Add green beans and continue simmering 5 minutes. Add cannellini and walnuts, and simmer 5 minutes more.

Serve sprinkled with dill. Serves 8–10.

The green, rolling Northeast Kingdom, so-called by Senator George Aiken in the 1940s, comprises the three most northeastern counties of the state. It is a somewhat remote, wildly beautiful place of lakes, forests, hills, and few people. Some say it is Vermont distilled to its essence.

Moroccan Lamb Stew

2½ pounds boneless lamb shoulder, cut in 1½-inch cubes
¼ cup olive oil
4 small yellow onions, quartered
Fresh ginger root, minced, or 2 teaspoons ground ginger
2 cloves garlic, crushed
¼ cup chopped parsley
1½ tablespoons salt, or less
¼ teaspoon turmeric
⅛ teaspoon pepper
1 cup tomatoes, undrained
1 cup raisins
½ cup blanched almonds
3½ tablespoons butter or margarine
2 hard-boiled eggs (optional)
3 cups cold water
1½ cups long-grain rice
Chopped parsley

In the early 19th century Vermont ranked first in the nation in sheep raising. Again, sheep farming is on the rise with a new emphasis on providing high-grade lamb for market.

Heat oil in a 5–6 quart Dutch oven. Brown lamb cubes over medium heat, ⅓ at a time. Remove. Add onions, ginger, and garlic. Sauté, stirring until onion is golden. Add parsley, 1 tablespoon salt, turmeric and pepper. Return lamb to pan and add tomatoes.

Place a piece of wax paper over casserole, then cover with lid. Bring to a boil and simmer, covered, for 1¼ hours, stirring occasionally.

Cover raisins with water and let stand.

In 2 tablespoons of butter, sauté almonds until golden. Peel eggs and chop fine, if using.

In a medium saucepan put 3 cups cold water, rice, 1½ teaspoons salt, and remaining butter. Bring to boil uncovered, reduce heat, and simmer, covered, 15–20 minutes or until no water remains. Drain raisins and stir into meat. Simmer covered 5 minutes.

Combine rice with lamb mixture in serving dish. Garnish with almonds, egg, and parsley. Serves 8.

Savory Lamb Shanks

A great way to cook the flavorful but inexpensive lamb shank. Reheats well, and will do you proud with family or guests.

4 lamb shanks
Olive oil as needed
2 tablespoons butter, optional
1 cup coarsely chopped onions
2 carrots, peeled and minced
4 cloves garlic, minced
¾ teaspoon dried rosemary
½ teaspoon dried thyme
Ground pepper
1 cup tomatoes, canned or fresh, chopped
2 tablespoons tomato paste
1 cup red wine
1 cup strong beef broth

Brown shanks in oil in a heavy skillet until they are brown on all sides. Transfer to a covered casserole along with most of the remaining oil.

Add onions, carrots, and spices to skillet, tossing over medium heat until onions are wilted. Add tomatoes, tomato paste, wine, and broth, bringing all to a boil. Pour over lamb shanks. Cover with foil, then lid, and bake at 300 degrees for about 2 hours.

If sauce is not thick enough at serving time, remove shanks and reduce liquid on top of stove. Serve with rice, barley or lentils. Serves 4.

To sauté without fat use 1 tablespoon of broth, vermouth, or water.

Lamb Pilaf

3 pounds (3 cups) cubed lamb
2 tablespoons butter
1 cup chopped onions
2 cups long-grain rice
1 cup dried currants
Salt and fresh ground pepper to taste
½ teaspoon cardamom
1 cup broken walnut meats
4 cups broth, chicken or beef
2 tomatoes, peeled and diced (1 cup)
½ cup parsley

Brown lamb in butter, remove and keep warm. Sauté onion until transparent, add rice and sauté a few minutes more. Add remaining ingredients and simmer for about 30 minutes or until liquid is absorbed.

Return lamb to the pot, and turn everything into a casserole. Heat thoroughly in oven or microwave. Serves 6–8.

Dead Creek Wildlife Refuge
Addison, Vermont

Mock Moussaka

Easier than making moussaka, but combines many of the same flavors.

1 large eggplant, about 1½ pounds
1½ pounds ground lamb or beef
½ cup olive oil
1 cup onion, minced
1 teaspoon garlic, minced
Freshly ground pepper to taste
1 tablespoon oregano
½ teaspoon cinnamon
4 cups (1 pound 12 ounce can) tomatoes in tomato paste or purée
1 egg
¾ cup Parmesan cheese, grated
1 cup bread crumbs

Don't peel eggplant if young. Cut into 1-inch cubes which should be about 6 cups. Brown meat and drain off fat. Heat the oil in a skillet, and add onion and garlic, stirring until onion is wilted. Add the meat and eggplant. Cook 10 minutes. Add the pepper, cinnamon, oregano, and tomatoes. Cook, stirring, 5 minutes. Add ¼ cup of the cheese and the slightly beaten egg.

Spoon the mixture into a casserole or baking dish. Sprinkle with a mixture of crumbs and the remaining cheese. Bake 15 minutes at 425° or until eggplant is done. Makes good leftovers. Serves 4–6.

What to do with the rest of a can of tomato paste when the recipe calls for only 2-tablespoons? Freeze it in plastic-wrapped, 2 tablespoon packets for future use.

Lamb and Ratatouille Casserole

2 pounds lamb shoulder cut in 1-inch cubes
2 tablespoons oil (more if needed)
2 medium onions, chopped
1 large clove garlic, minced

Sauté lamb in small batches until well browned. Remove from skillet. Sauté onions and garlic until golden. Return lamb to skillet and mix well.

Mix the following ingredients:

½ cup raw rice
1 pound potatoes, peeled and thinly sliced
1 teaspoon salt
1½ teaspoons curry powder
Several grinds of black pepper
1 (14 ounce) can artichoke hearts, drained and rinsed
2 (1 pound) cans tomatoes, undrained
1 medium zucchini, sliced

In a 3-quart casserole layer ⅓ of meat mixture, then ⅓ other mixture, repeating twice. Bake covered for 2 hours at 350 degrees or until lamb and potatoes are tender. Serves 6–8.

Lamb Steak on the Grill

Leg of lamb sliced 1½ inches thick
½ cup soy sauce
½ cup dry red wine
½ cup olive oil
¼ cup ginger root, peeled and chopped
2 large cloves garlic, minced
1 tablespoon molasses

Mix ingredients for marinade, add lamb slices, and marinate at least 3 hours. Grill over charcoal 6 minutes on one side and 4 minutes on the other. We like it a little pink.

Grilled Marinated Flank Steak

2 pound flank steak
3 tablespoons olive oil
3 tablespoons soy sauce
½ onion, minced
1 teaspoon parsley, minced
1 teaspoon ground thyme
1 teaspoon marjoram
Dash black pepper
2 tablespoons butter
2 tablespoons chives, chopped
2 tablespoons bleu cheese

Combine oil, soy sauce, onion, and seasonings for marinade. Marinate steak 2 to 3 hours or overnight in the refrigerator. When ready to serve, place on grill, brush with marinade, and grill 3 minutes per side or until desired doneness. Spread with a mixture of butter, chives, and bleu cheese. Slice thinly on the diagonal and serve.

Marinated Flank Steak

2-pound flank steak
2 tablespoons tomato paste
3–4 teaspoons soy sauce
1 tablespoon vegetable oil
1 clove garlic, minced
1½ teaspoons oregano
1 teaspoon salt
¼–½ teaspoon freshly ground pepper

Combine all ingredients for marinade. Beat to thicken. Paint both sides of steak with marinade. Roll up jellyroll fashion, and wrap in aluminum foil or plastic wrap. Marinate at least 1 hour. Unroll meat, broil or grill until pink in center. Slice in thin strips at an angle to the grain.

The marinated steak may be frozen, tightly wrapped, and thawed and cooked later.

Grilled Pot Roast "Steak"

1 slice of pot roast about 2 inches thick (chuck is ideal)
Prepared mustard
Salt

Spread mustard thickly on both sides of the roast. Cover with salt. Cook on a hot grill as you would steak. Scrape off any leftover salt and mustard before serving.

This really works! The pot roast is tenderized as it cooks and you'd swear you were eating steak.

Saucy Pot Roast

A great second-day dish. Microwave slices of the meat and gravy for 2 minutes. Wonderful.

2½–3 pounds boneless pot roast
1 tablespoon bacon fat
2 medium carrots, coarsely chopped
2 medium potatoes, coarsely chopped
2 medium onions, coarsely chopped
2 cloves garlic, minced
1 cup red wine
1 cup beef bouillon
½ teaspoon thyme
2 bay leaves
Salt and pepper, to taste

Brown meat in bacon fat. Add chopped vegetables and sauté. Add remaining ingredients, and simmer 3–4 hours.

Remove meat and bay leaves. Degrease, then dump everything else in food processor and purée. Reheat this sauce with meat, and serve with noodles or potatoes. Serves 6.

In thickening power, 1 tablespoon of cornstarch equals 2 tablespoons of flour.

Beef Ragout
with Sour Cream

2 pounds round steak or chuck cut in 1½-inch cubes
2 large onions, sliced
1 tablespoon curry powder
⅔ cup red wine
⅔ cup consommé
Salt and pepper, to taste
⅔ cup sour cream
1 tablespoon horseradish

Combine beef, onions, curry powder, wine, consommé, salt, and pepper in a large pot. Bring to a boil on top of the stove. Cover and bake in a 325-degree oven for 1½ –2 hours until meat is very tender.

Move pot to top of stove, add sour cream and horseradish, and reheat. Do not boil. Serves 4–6.

This is especially good with buttered noodles.

Thetford Center, Vt.

Beef Stew with Olives

3 pounds beef chuck cut in 1½-inch pieces
¼ pound salt pork, diced
2 tablespoons olive oil
3 medium tomatoes, peeled, seeded, and chopped
1 cup brown stock or bouillon
3 or 4 large strips of orange peel
1 clove garlic, mashed
2 bay leaves
¾ teaspoon marjoram
¾ teaspoon thyme
½ teaspoon saffron threads
3 medium onions, sliced
1 cup dry red wine
¼ cup brandy
12 green olives, pitted and halved
12 soft, oil-cured black olives, pitted and halved

Dry chuck pieces. In a heavy skillet, brown salt pork in olive oil, and transfer with slotted spoon to heavy casserole. In remaining fat brown chuck, a few pieces at a time, over moderately high heat. Transfer it with slotted spoon to casserole and add tomatoes, stock, orange peel, and spices.

In fat remaining in skillet sauté onion slices until softened and add to casserole. Discard any fat in the skillet and pour in the wine and brandy. Be careful adding the brandy as it is flammable. Bring to a near-boil and cook over high heat, stirring in brown bits clinging to bottom for several minutes. Pour this sauce over meat, cover casserole tightly, and bake at 350 degrees for 1½ hours.

Blanch olives in boiling water for five minutes and add to the stew. Continue baking for another hour or until meat is very tender. Serves 6–8.

Portuguese Meat and Vegetables

3 pounds beef, cut in small pieces with fat removed
Olive oil
1 tablespoon mixed spices (oregano, chopped garlic, bay leaf, thyme, plus others
    if desired)
Salt and pepper to taste
1 pound small onions
3 pounds peas
1¼ pounds carrots, cut in small chunks
½ cup beer
1 tablespoon butter or margarine
Parsley, chopped

Mix meat with a small amount of olive oil and stir in the mixed spices and salt and pepper. Marinate in fridge for at least half an hour.

Place meat and a third of the onions in a kettle with an inch or two of water. Bring to a boil, cover, reduce heat and cook for about an hour. Add peas, carrots, and remaining onions. You may add any other vegetables you wish; tomatoes are good.

Add beer, and continue to cook for another hour or less. Before serving add butter and chopped parsley. Be careful not to scorch. Reheats easily for excellent second meal. Serves 10–12.

Meats

Meatloaf with Cranberries

1½ pounds ground beef
½ pound ground ham
¾ cup milk
¾ cup oatmeal
2 eggs
1 teaspoon salt
A few grinds of pepper
1 small onion, minced

Mix everything together lightly but thoroughly.

½ cup cranberry sauce
¼ cup brown sugar
3 bay leaves

Mix together the cranberry sauce and brown sugar and spread in the bottom of a loaf pan. Put meat mixture on top. Press three bay leaves in the top of the loaf and bake at 350 degrees for 1¼ hours. Remove bay leaves and unmold. The cranberries and brown sugar make a topping.

Add fiber to meat loaves or meat balls by adding rolled oats or oat bran.

Best-Ever Meatloaf

1½ pounds ground chuck
1 cup fresh bread crumbs
1 onion, chopped
1 egg
1 teaspoon salt, or less
¼ teaspoon pepper
½ (8 ounce) can tomato sauce

Sauce:

½ cup water
3 tablespoons vinegar
3 tablespoons brown sugar
2 tablespoons mustard
2 tablespoons Worcestershire sauce
1½ (8 ounce) cans tomato sauce

Mix loaf ingredients, form into loaf, and put on roasting pan.

Mix sauce ingredients thoroughly and pour over meat; or reserve some, simmer it 10 minutes and serve with the meat loaf. Bake at 350 degrees for 1¼ hours, basting with sauce. Let loaf sit for about 5 minutes before slicing.

Luscious Liver

Marinate any good-looking liver in commercially bottled teriyaki sauce, then cook quickly over charcoal. You'll be surprised. Very good.

Corned Beef

Corned beef
Vegetables as desired
3 tablespoons brown sugar
Ginger ale
½ cup Dijon-style mustard

On the day before you plan to serve it simmer the corned beef as directed until it is done. It will cut better if cooked ahead. Reserve the broth.

Before dinner place the beef on a broiler rack with warm water underneath. A piece of foil under the beef loosely crimped around its sides will keep the juices where you want them. Rub the meat on all sides with ½ cup Dijon-style mustard mixed with three tablespoons brown sugar. Then dribble ginger ale over it every 15 minutes or so during baking. Bake at 350 for about 45 minutes.

Simmer the vegetables you have chosen in the reserved beef broth. If you prefer not to serve with the traditional boiled vegetables, it is good with scalloped potatoes.

New England Boiled Dinner

A chilly fall night on the farm and New England boiled dinner—a combination we never forget. The vegetables were harvested from our own garden and Mother most likely corned her own brisket of beef. Now we buy the ingredients at the supermarket, but the finished dish still takes us "home."

Corned brisket of beef or corned round of beef (harder to find but better)
Rutabagas or turnips
Carrots
Potatoes
Onions
Beets
Cabbage

Quantities depend on how many people you are serving and how much you want left over for Red Flannel Hash. Plan a half-pound of corned beef, 2 small onions, 2 small beets, 1 wedge of cabbage, and 2 good-sized chunks of the other vegetables per person.

In deep kettle cover meat with water, bring to a boil, cover, and simmer 3 hours. Cut cabbage wedges, peel the vegetables, and cut into 2-inch chunks where appropriate. Add rutabagas, carrots, and potatoes to the meat pot. Cook beets and onions each in their own pot. Bring meat pot to a boil and simmer about 45 minutes or until vegetables are tender. Add cabbage for the last 20 minutes.

To serve, place the meat on a large platter and surround it with all the vegetables. It is traditional to serve homemade bread, pickles, horseradish, and vinegar to sprinkle on the cabbage.

The trick to making smooth gravy or sauce is simple: remove the flour-fat mixture from the heat before adding the liquid. Whisk liquid and roux together until all is smooth, and only then return saucepan to heat. Bring to a boil, whisk continually, and allow to thicken to desired consistency. Truly foolproof.

Veal Piccata

½ cup butter
2 pounds round of veal, sliced thin
Flour for dredging
½ cup lemon juice
½ cup sauterne
Salt, minced garlic, pepper, to taste
1 (16 ounce) can mushrooms, drained
12 scallions, chopped
½ cup Parmesan cheese, grated

Melt butter in skillet. Flour veal and brown in butter for 1 minute on each side. Remove to oven-proof dish large enough to hold veal in single, overlapping layer.

Mix together lemon juice, sauterne, and seasonings. Pour over veal. Sprinkle mushrooms and onions on top. Cover and bake 30 minutes at 350 degrees. Sprinkle cheese over it before serving. Serves 8.

Veal Casino

Equally good using pork medallions or chicken breasts.

4 veal chops
Flour to dust
½ cup olive oil
2 tablespoons butter
8 plum tomatoes, chopped
2 large artichoke hearts, sliced
6 green olives, chopped
Dash of bitters
½ teaspoon dry mustard
4 scallions, chopped
Black pepper
Red or white wine or Marsala, garlic, basil (optional)

Sauté floured chops in butter and olive oil, 4 minutes per side. Turn only once.

To make sauce add the rest of the ingredients, and sauté 6–8 minutes.
Serves 4.

Add 2 teaspoons powdered coffee to colorless gravy to make it darker and not change taste.

Carne de Porco a Alentejana

(Pork and Mussels, from Portugal)

1 pound lean pork, cut into small pieces
1 ounce oil or other shortening
1 tablespoon olive oil
2 onions, chopped
2 cloves garlic, chopped
2 tomatoes, chopped
2 bay leaves
Salt, to taste
Freshly ground pepper
1 tablespoon paprika
½ cup white wine
1 pound mussels

You will notice several recipes in this book from Portugal. "Not very Vermont," you say, which is certainly true except that the Episcopal Diocese of Vermont has as its Companion Diocese the Diocese of Lusitania, or Portugal. We have enjoyed a considerable amount of back-and-forth with our friends across the Atlantic. Among its fruits are these recipes, contributed by Portuguese Episcopalians, in Portuguese, and translated here in Vermont in what we trust is correct and usable form.

Fry pork in shortening until meat is almost cooked. Set aside. In another skillet heat olive oil and sauté onions and garlic until they are soft and transparent. Add tomatoes, bay leaves, salt, pepper, and paprika. Cook about 10 minutes. Add mussels, pork, and wine. Cover and cook until mussels open. Serve with crusty bread. Serves 4.

Note: If you are fortunate enough to find clams no bigger than a quarter, try them also.

One-Step Pork Chop and Rice Dinner

4 thick loin pork chops
1 cup rice
4 thick slices onion
4 thick slices fresh tomatoes
4 thick slices green pepper
2½ cups beef bouillon
½ teaspoon marjoram
¼ teaspoon thyme (optional)
Salt and pepper

Sauté chops on both sides, and place in low casserole. Put ⅛ cup dry rice on each chop topped by 1 slice each of onion, tomato, and pepper. Add more rice in the spaces between chops.

Pour bouillon over all, sprinkle with seasonings. Cover and bake at 350 degrees for about 1 hour. Check, and if it is getting dry, add more bouillon or a little water. Serves 4.

Use twice as much fresh as dried herbs.

Sweet and Sour Pork

2 pounds boned, lean pork
1 each green, red, yellow, and orange pepper
1 onion
1 egg, lightly beaten
½ cup cornstarch
6 tablespoons oil
¼ pound sugar peas or snow peas

Cut pork, peppers, and onion in chunks. Dip pork chunks in egg, then roll in corn starch. Brown and cook 5–7 minutes in 2 tablespoons oil. Stir-fry peppers and onion in oil. Stir-fry peapods in oil. We think the quality of the dish is better if the 3 things are stir-fried crisp-tender separately, but they can be done in 1 large pan, especially if you have a wok. Keep warm.

Sauce:

½ cup vinegar
½ cup ketchup
¼ cup pineapple juice
½ cup brown sugar
¼ cup cornstarch
2 tablespoons soy sauce

Combine ingredients and cook over low heat, stirring constantly, until sauce thickens. Combine with stir-fried meat and vegetables and serve over hot rice. Serves 6.

Hot Chinese Pork and Cabbage

Regulate the firepower by how much red pepper you use. Start with a little and taste.

½ pound lean pork
2 cups water
1 teaspoon sherry
2 tablespoons ginger root, minced
3 tablespoons oil
3 cups sliced green cabbage
¼ cup bean paste
3 tablespoons soy sauce
1–2 teaspoons crushed red pepper flakes
2 cloves garlic, minced

Simmer pork with the water, sherry, and 1 tablespoon minced ginger for 15 minutes or until cooked through. Let cool in the pan, and reserve cooking liquid. Cut pork into 2-inch x ½-inch strips.

Place half the oil in wok or skillet over medium heat, and add cabbage. Stir-fry about 1 minute until cabbage is partially translucent.

Push cabbage to side, add remaining oil, then add remaining ginger, bean paste, soy sauce, pepper flakes, garlic, pork, and pork liquid. Stir-fry another 2 minutes until all is mixed with cabbage. Serve on rice or linguine. Serves 3–4.

Sausages in White Wine

1 pound country sausages
1 tablespoon butter or margarine
1 shallot, minced
1½ tablespoons flour
1½ cups dry white wine

Prick sausage skins and cook slowly in skillet. When done, remove sausages and pour off all the fat.

Put butter or margarine in skillet, add shallot, and blend in flour. Cook 2 to 3 minutes. Add wine and cook 20 minutes. Return sausages to pan to warm in sauce. Serve with mashed potatoes. Serves 2–3.

Tourtière

This pork pie is a traditional French Canadian dish on Christmas Eve, usually served to family and friends after midnight mass. It has become a tradition in many Vermont families as well, and says "Christmas Eve" to many of us.

3 pounds ground pork
6 slices bread, crusts removed, cubed
3 cups water
¾ cup or more chopped onions
1 teaspoon cinnamon
½ teaspoon ground cloves
Salt and pepper, to taste
2 batches double pie crust

This makes 2 9-inch pies. At least 1 day before serving, cook meat in kettle with water until the meat loses its pink color. Break up any lumps. Add bread, spices and onion. Simmer about 1½ hours, stirring often. (You may wish to start with less cinnamon and cloves; taste during the simmering and add as you go along.) Refrigerate overnight.

Next day remove what you can of the hardened pork fat, divide between 2 lined pie plates, cover with top crusts, sealing rims well. Make several vents in top crust. Pies may be frozen at this point after being well wrapped in foil. Thaw before baking. Bake in a 450-degree oven about 45 minutes, or until nice and brown. Let stand before trying to cut; serve warm. Serves 12-14.

A planning tip: Most of our dietary fat comes from meats, sauces, and fried foods. If we cut down on those, there's room for dessert—within reason.

Ham Loaf

1 pound ham, ground
1 pound pork, ground
1 egg, beaten
2–3 slices bread, in small pieces
1 small onion, chopped
1 tablespoon dried parsley
1 tablespoon lemon juice
Dash each pepper and ground cloves
1 teaspoon brown sugar

In a large bowl combine beaten egg, bread, onion, parsley, lemon juice, pepper, cloves, and brown sugar. Add meats. Combine well and shape into loaf. Sprinkle bottom of loaf pan with more ground cloves and brown sugar. Place shaped loaf in pan. Sprinkle top with still more ground cloves and brown sugar. Can be refrigerated at this point. When ready to serve, bake in 350-degree oven for 1½ hours. Serves 6.

Roast Venison Barbecue

Ham of a deer
½ cup vinegar
⅛ cup brown sugar
Salt
Flour
½ cup butter, melted
1 cup water
½ cup ketchup
2 tablespoons Worcestershire sauce
Clove of garlic, crushed
5 tablespoons onion, chopped

Rub the ham of deer with a mixture of vinegar and brown sugar. Then rub with salt, dredge with flour, and brown on all sides. Place on a rack in a roasting pan and add a small amount of water to bottom of the pan.

To make a sauce combine the remaining ingredients. Pour over roast and baste occasionally. Cook 30 minutes per pound at 350 degrees.

Hunting is a popular sport which provides fresh venison, pheasant, and partridge for many tables. Several Vermont towns have widely renowned game suppers in the fall which feature exotic fare, and you might find on your plate wild boar roast, bear sausage, or moose burgers.

Vegetables

Newbury, Vermont

Garden Paella

3 tablespoons salad oil
1 cup raw long-grain rice
1 cup chopped onion
1½ cup shredded carrots
1 red or green pepper, diced
3 cloves garlic, crushed
1 teaspoon paprika
½ teaspoon salt
⅛ teaspoon each oregano, cayenne, thyme
1 cup chicken broth
3 cups broccoli flowerets
2 cups cauliflower flowerets
1 (16 ounce) can tomatoes, drained and chopped

In a large skillet heat 2 tablespoons oil, add rice, and cook, stirring occasionally, until opaque. Add remaining oil, onions, carrots, pepper, and garlic. Sauté for 2 minutes. Add paprika, cayenne, salt, and herbs. Stir in broth. Bring to a boil and cover. Simmer 10 minutes. Then add broccoli, cauliflower, and tomatoes. Continue simmering until all is tender. May be served hot or cold. To reheat, bake in a 350-degree oven until hot. Serves 6.

Summer Saturday mornings are the time for farmers' markets in towns all over the state. Baskets of butter-and-sugar corn picked at dawn sit next to big tomatoes ready for slicing, and there are often baked goods, yarn made from the wool of local sheep, cut flowers, and potted herbs, as well as many old friends to share a word with.

Fresh Asparagus Microwave

After the typically long, hard winter of the North Country, asparagus, above all other vegetables, signals spring. It grows wild in various areas of the state, and searching it out is a special pleasure for the outdoorsman-cook. This is the easiest way we know to preserve its delicate taste and texture.

Clean and prepare the desired amount of asparagus. Have ready a glass container of sufficient size to hold your aspargus loosely upright. Fill the container half full of water and bring to the boil in the microwave. Remove container from the oven, stand prepared asparagus on end in the boiling water, return to the oven and microwave for 2–4 minutes or to desired degree of tenderness. There you are. Dress with drawn butter and fresh lemon juice, and salute the spring!

Cauliflower and Peas

1 medium head cauliflower
1 (10 ounce) box frozen peas, thawed, or equivalent fresh
2 tablespoons butter
2 tablespoons flour
1½ cups milk
¾ cup grated Cheddar cheese
¼ cup sherry
1 teaspoon salt
¼ teaspoon pepper

Break cauliflower into flowerets and steam until crisp-tender. Blanch peas, if using fresh.

Melt butter in saucepan. Stir in flour and cook slightly. Add milk and sherry and stir until thickened. Add cheese and stir until melted. Add peas, salt and pepper. Pour over cauliflower. Best if served right away. Serves 6.

Broccoli in Yogurt Sauce

2 pounds fresh broccoli
3 egg yolks
½ teaspoon cornstarch
1 cups plain yogurt
2 teaspoons Dijon-style mustard
1 large clove garlic, crushed
Salt and freshly ground pepper
Lemon juice

Remove tough outer leaves of broccoli and cut 1 inch off the base. Quarter branches lengthwise up through the flowerheads. Set aside.

In the top of a double boiler, combine the yolks and cornstarch. Whisk until well blended. Add yogurt, mustard, and garlic and place over simmering water. Whisk mixture until it thickens and heavily coats the whisk. Do not let it come to a boil. Season with salt and pepper and a large dash of lemon juice. Keep covered over warm but not boiling water.

In a large pan, bring 3–4 quarts of water to a boil. Add prepared broccoli and boil uncovered for 7 minutes. Drain and arrange in serving dish. Serve sauce separately. Serves 6–8.

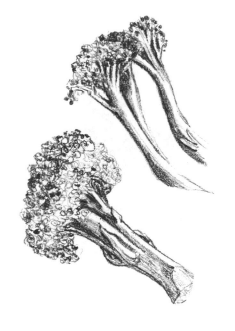

Old-Fashioned Baked Beans

2 pounds dried navy beans
2 quarts cold water
1 medium onion, sliced
1 tablespoon salt
4 teaspoons cider vinegar
1 teaspoon prepared mustard
2 tablespoons brown sugar or maple syrup
½ cup molasses
¼ cup tomato ketchup
1/16 teaspoon black pepper
Hot water, if needed
½ pound salt pork, sliced

Sort and rinse beans. Soak overnight in cold water. Next day, heat and simmer (do not boil) for 30 minutes.

Slice onion in the bottom of a 10-cup casserole. Combine the next 7 ingredients with the beans and pour into the casserole—liquid should cover beans. Add more, if necessary. Push pork slices into beans. Bake, covered, in a slow oven (250 degrees) for 7–8 hours.

Note: You can use any kind of dry bean, omit salt, and add maple syrup to taste.

Green Beans, Red Peppers, and Baby Onions

A beautiful dish, as good as it is lovely to look at.

1 (10 ounce) box baby pearl onions, blanched and peeled
1½ pound green beans, trimmed and left whole
1 large red sweet pepper, thinly sliced in strips
2 tablespoons margarine or cooking oil
Hot pepper oil or sesame oil to taste, if desired
Salt and pepper to taste, if desired

Steam green beans until crisp-tender. Drain and set aside. In a large skillet, sauté onions and red pepper in oil or margarine, adding a few drops of hot oil if you wish, until pepper slices are tender and onions are lightly browned.

Add beans to skillet and toss to mix. Season to taste with salt and pepper. Serves 6–8.

Herbed Green Beans

¼ cup margarine or butter
¾ cup minced onion
1 clove garlic, minced
½ cup minced celery
2 tablespoons sesame seeds
¼ teaspoon dried rosemary
¼ teaspoon dried basil
3 teaspoons salt, or to taste
1 teaspoon minced parsley
1 pound green beans

Melt margarine in a saucepan. Sauté onion, garlic, celery, and sesame seeds for about 5 minutes. Add rosemary, basil, salt and parsley. Simmer everything for about 10 minutes. This sauce can be prepared early in the day.

At serving time, cook beans to desired degree of doneness—crisp-tender seems about right—and toss with the sauce, which has been heated through. Serve at once. Serves 4.

Keep a container in the freezer for left-over cooked vegetables to add to soups and stews.

136

Lemon Parsley Carrots

1 bunch of carrots, scraped and julienned
¼ cup water
½ teaspoon salt
½ teaspoon grated lemon peel
2 teaspoons fresh lemon juice
1 tablespoon sugar
1 tablespoon snipped parsley
2 tablespoons butter or margarine

Cook julienned carrots until just tender. Drain thoroughly and set aside in a warm place.

Combine remaining ingredients in a medium saucepan. Heat until butter melts and sugar dissolves. Add carrots and toss well. Serve hot. Serves 4.

Baked Carrots

4 cups grated carrots (about 9 medium)
2 teaspoons sugar
1 teaspoon salt
½ teaspoon ground pepper
4 tablespoons butter or margarine

Heat oven to 400 degrees. Place carrots in a 4-cup casserole and sprinkle seasonings over them. Dot with butter, cover, and bake for 30 minutes. Serves 6.

Cucumbers in Cream

A surprising, different, and delicious dish—try it.

3 large cucumbers, peeled, quartered lengthwise, and cut into 1-inch pieces
5 tablespoons butter
Salt and pepper, to taste
¼ cup sour cream
¼ cup heavy cream
Juice of half a lemon

Heat oven to 325 degrees. Simmer cucumbers in water to cover for 5 minutes. Drain well.

In a casserole large enough to hold cucumbers, melt the butter. Add the well-drained cucumbers and season to taste. Cover casserole and bake for 20 minutes.

Meanwhile, combine the creams. After 20 minutes in the oven, add the creams to the cucumbers and bake, uncovered, 5 minutes more. Sprinkle lemon juice over all. Serves 6.

Fiddlehead Ferns

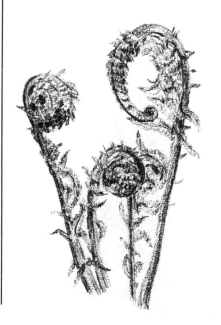

1 pound fiddleheads
Butter
Salt and pepper, to taste

Clean fiddleheads (see page 25). The easiest and most usual way to cook fiddleheads is to steam them for about 8 minutes, then serve with butter, salt and pepper. One pound serves 4.

They are also good cold in a vinaigrette dressing or stir-fried with shrimp or chicken.

Vegetables

Mushrooms Florentine

2 packages (10 ounce) frozen chopped spinach, thawed and squeezed dry
½ cup chopped onion
6 tablespoons butter
Salt and pepper, to taste
1 cup shredded Cheddar cheese
¼ cup bread crumbs
1 pound fresh mushrooms, washed and sliced

Spread spinach evenly over the bottom of a shallow casserole. Sprinkle the onions over it, along with 2 tablespoons melted butter, salt, pepper, and ½ cup shredded cheese.

Sauté sliced mushrooms in remaining butter until brown and most of the moisture has evaporated. Spoon over spinach-cheese mixture. Sprinkle with remaining cheese mixed with bread crumbs. Bake in a 350-degree oven for 20–30 minutes. Serves 6–8 as accompaniment to meat or poultry.

Bermudas Glacé

6 Bermuda onions
2 tablespoons margarine
¼ cup honey
½ teaspoon paprika
½ teaspoon salt
⅛ teaspoon pepper
3 tablespoons water

Heat oven to 350 degrees. Peel and halve onions. Place cut side up in a casserole with a cover. Top with remaining ingredients, cover, and bake for about 1½ hours. Baste occasionally. Serves 12.

May be prepared ahead and reheated in the microwave.

Mushrooms stored in a paper bag will absorb moisture and keep fresh.

Potatoes Hashed in Cream

4 baking potatoes
3 tablespoons butter
1 teaspoon flour
1 cup heavy cream
1 teaspoon salt
1 teaspoon pepper
2 tablespoons chopped onion
¼ teaspoon nutmeg

Bake potatoes until soft but still firm. Peel, cube, and set aside. Melt 2 tablespoons butter. Stir in flour and gradually add cream. Stir sauce until it thickens. Add salt, pepper, onion, and nutmeg. Gently mix in the cubed potatoes.

Place in a greased baking dish. Dot with remaining tablespoon of butter and bake in a 350-degree oven for 30 minutes, covered. May be prepared ahead and reheated at serving time. Serves 4–6.

Herb-Baked Potatoes

6 cups diced potatoes
1 medium onion, chopped
¾ cup chopped celery
¼ cup melted butter
1 teaspoon salt
3 tablespoons minced parsley
Fresh ground pepper
¾ teaspoon poultry seasoning

Cook the potatoes in a small amount of water in a covered saucepan until just tender. Drain well. Mix with remaining ingredients and place in an oven-proof casserole. Bake covered for 30 minutes at 375 degrees, then uncovered for an additional 10 minutes. Serves 6.

Baked Pumpkin

Clearly for your more dramatic moments—an interesting and delicious way to serve a vegetable.

1 small pumpkin
2 tablespoons honey
2 tablespoons apple cider
2 tablespoons melted butter or margarine

Preheat oven to 350 degrees. Wash pumpkin well, place on a flat oven-proof dish and bake for about 1½ hours.

Remove from oven and cut a hole about 4 inches in diameter in top of pumpkin. Remove the "hat" and scrape out seeds and strings. Leave flesh intact.

Mix together the honey, cider and butter and pour into pumpkin, "basting" flesh as best you can. Return to oven for 35–40 minutes longer, basting occasionally. (A bulb baster does the trick here.)

Serve pumpkin whole, scooping out flesh in individual portions at the table, or cut like a melon. In any case, pour a bit of cider sauce over each serving and enjoy.

Easy Spinach Casserole

2 cups wide noodles, cooked and drained
1 package chopped spinach, thawed and squeezed dry
1 cup Swiss cheese, grated

2 tablespoons butter or margarine
2 tablespoons flour
1 cup milk
¼ teaspoon salt
⅛ teaspoon pepper

Melt butter or margarine in a small, heavy saucepan. Stir in flour and cook, stirring, for a few minutes—until flour loses raw taste and mixture is smooth. Remove from heat and slowly pour in milk, stirring with a whisk as you do so. Return to heat and cook, stirring, until sauce thickens. Add seasoning to taste.

In a 1–½-quart casserole, layer ½ the noodles, ½ the cheese, the spinach, the rest of the noodles, the rest of the cheese. Pour sauce over all and bake at 350 degrees for about 30 minutes. Serves 4.

Butternut Squash
with Ginger and Garlic

1 butternut squash, about 2 pounds
½ teaspoon salt
2 tablespoons butter
2 tablespoons each finely minced fresh ginger and garlic
2–3 tablespoons fresh minced parsley and/or chives

Cut squash in half lengthwise and scrape out seeds and strings. Peel outer skin with a vegetable peeler. Dice squash into 1-inch chunks, and place in a pan with water almost to cover. Add salt, bring to a boil, cover, and simmer for about 20 minutes, or until squash is just tender. Don't overcook.

Drain cooking water into another pan, adding the butter, ginger and garlic. Boil rapidly to reduce liquid. When well-reduced, add squash, parsley and/or chives, and serve. Serves 6–8.

Squash au Gratin

1½ pounds yellow summer squash, sliced
1 large onion, sliced
¼ teaspoon pepper
2 tablespoons butter or margarine
½ pound sharp Cheddar cheese, shredded

Preheat oven to 400 degrees. Cook squash in lightly salted water until tender-crisp. Drain well. In a buttered casserole, layer squash, onion rings, seasoning, butter and cheese, ending with cheese. Bake 15–20 minutes or until it bubbles. Serves 4.

If parsley is washed in hot water instead of cold, it keeps its flavor and is easier to chop.

Cherry Tomatoes with Basil

1 (pint) box cherry tomatoes, washed and dried
1–2 tablespoons olive oil
⅛ teaspoon garlic salt, or to taste
½ teaspoon dried basil *or* 1–2 tablespoons chopped fresh

In a non-stick skillet, heat olive oil with basil and garlic salt. Add tomatoes, and shake pan to roll them well in oil and herbs while heating through. Do not overcook.

Serve as side dish or garnish. Serves 4–6.

Onions with Broccoli and Cheddar

6 medium onions or 3 Spanish onions, halved crosswise
3 cups broccoli flowerets, steamed until just tender
½ cup (or more) grated sharp Cheddar cheese
⅓ cup good-quality light mayonnaise
1 tablespoon lemon juice

Gently parboil peeled onions or halves for 10–12 minutes, until they are tender but retain some shape. Don't worry if they separate—you can re-form them later. When drained and cooled, remove the centers, leaving shells thick enough to hold their shape but with room for ample filling—use your judgment here.

Chop onion centers to equal 1 cup. Chop cooked broccoli coarsely and combine with onion. Gently mix in remaining ingredients, adjusting seasonings to your taste. Spoon this mixture into the onion shells, mounding it nicely. Sprinkle with grated Parmesan if you like.

Place filled onions in a buttered oven dish and bake uncovered for 20 minutes in a 375-degree oven. Serves 6.

These recipes for stuffed vegetables are labor intensive and not for everyday perhaps. But they are not hard, can be done ahead, and reheated in the microwave. Exact times will vary according to your particular microwave, but start on full power at 3 minutes for the tomatoes, 4 minutes for the onions, and adjust as necessary. The vegetables will not lose their shape and will make a smashing addition to your buffet table.

Tomatoes Stuffed with Spinach

In just about every case frozen chopped spinach can be substituted for fresh, using 1 10-ounce box for each pound or so of fresh. Remember to press out as much liquid as possible from the thawed spinach, and bear in mind that the flavor will not be quite as special. It is our opinion that the extra time involved for the fresh can be well worth it in terms of enhanced flavor.

5 or 6 medium, firm tomatoes
2 (10 ounce) bags leaf spinach, washed and stemmed
1 medium onion, finely minced
1 tablespoon margarine
½ cup grated Parmesan cheese
Generous pinch each of basil and oregano
Freshly ground pepper
Bread crumbs—2 pieces bread toasted crisply then crumbled in blender

To prepare tomatoes: Core and stem, removing pulp, seeds, and most of interior meat, but leaving a firm case which will keep its shape. Save the pulp for later use. Salt the insides of the tomatoes lightly and invert to drain while you prepare the filling.

Heat oven to 350 degrees. Cook spinach in the water which clings to it from the cleaning process. Cook for about 3 minutes, stirring until spinach wilts and loses bulk. Remove from stove, drain, and squeeze out all the water. Chop fine.

Sauté onion in 1 tablespoon margarine until translucent. Add remaining margarine and spinach; sauté another few minutes. Add remaining ingredients, mixing thoroughly. Add a bit of the tomato pulp if the mixture seems too dry. Taste and adjust seasonings to your liking.

Fill prepared tomato shells with spinach mixture—this is easiest done by hand. Tamp filling down well and mound tops nicely. Place on buttered baking sheet or dish and bake for 8–10 minutes, until tomatoes are soft but not mushy. Serves 5–6.

Pasta-Filled Tomatoes

Not for cholesterol watchers—the cream is the key. But beautiful and tasty.

8 medium tomatoes
Salt and pepper
¼ pound spinach pasta—linguine, noodles, or spaghetti
1 cup heavy cream
1 cup light cream
½ teaspoon ground thyme—or other herb of your choice
½ teaspoon salt
⅛ teaspoon pepper
Freshly grated Parmesan cheese

To prepare tomatoes: Core and stem, removing pulp, seeds, and most of the interior meat but leaving a firm case which will keep its shape. Season the shells with salt and pepper and invert to drain.

Preheat the oven to 350 degrees. Cook pasta in boiling salted water according to package directions until al dente. Drain well.

In a medium-sized saucepan, heat all the cream. Add ground herb, salt, and pepper. Add drained pasta and simmer slowly until cream is absorbed—about 15 minutes. Stir from time to time and taste for seasoning.

While the pasta is cooking gently, place tomato shells in an ungreased shallow pan and bake for about 5 minutes, or until heated through but not mushy.

Fill shells with pasta and sprinkle with Parmesan. Bake a few minutes more and serve. Serves 8.

Gilfeather Turnips

This is a unique Vermont vegetable, developed by farmer John Gilfeather of Wardsboro in the early 20th century and sold by him each fall around the southeastern part of the state. They are mild, rather sweet, creamy white, and best after a frost. Today you may find a roadside market around Dummerston or Brattleboro that sells them in the fall, or you can grow your own from seed usually available from Agway in Brattleboro.

To cook Gilfeathers:

Peel, dice, and steam them until tender. Serve with butter and salt and pepper to taste.

Or

Purée cooked Gilfeathers in your food processor and mix half and half with mashed potatoes for an especially flavorful, traditional Thanksgiving dish.

Or

Cut into strips when turnips are very fresh and use, raw, with a dip.

Zucchini-Tomato Bake

¼ cup oil
1 clove garlic, minced
4 medium zucchini, sliced
¼ teaspoon dried oregano, or 1 teaspoon minced fresh
¼ teaspoon dried basil, or 1 teaspoon minced fresh
½ cup grated Cheddar cheese
½ cup grated Parmesan cheese
4 medium tomatoes, peeled and sliced
Salt and pepper, to taste
½ cup bread crumbs
2 tablespoons melted butter

Preheat oven to 350 degrees. Heat oil in skillet, add garlic, and cook at medium heat until garlic browns. Remove garlic. Sauté zucchini in the flavored oil. Combine seasonings and cheeses in a separate bowl.

In a greased 1½-quart baking dish, place alternate layers of zucchini and sliced tomatoes, sprinkling each layer with salt, pepper, and seasoning-cheese mixture. Combine bread crumbs with melted butter and sprinkle over top of casserole. Bake about 20–25 minutes until crumbs are brown. Serves 4–6.

Cooking fruits and vegetables softens the plant cell wall but does not change the dietary fiber. Grinding, mashing, or blending does decrease it.

Zucchini and Peppers with Lemon Crumbs

4 cups (about 2 pounds) zucchini, cut in ½-inch slices
2 or 3 red peppers, cut in rings
4 tablespoons butter or margarine
1 teaspoon lemon pepper (on spice shelf at your market)
½ teaspoon salt
1 cup soft bread crumbs
1 tablespoon grated lemon rind

Heat oven to 400 degrees. In a large skillet, sauté zucchini and pepper rings in 2 tablespoons butter until tender. Add lemon pepper and salt, and stir until well mixed.

In another skillet brown bread crumbs in remaining butter and add lemon rind.

Spread vegetables in lightly greased casserole dish. Sprinkle crumb mixture over them and bake for about 10 minutes. Serves 4–6.

You may substitute 2 cups seeded, chopped tomatoes for the red peppers.

Pita Pizza Pronto

2 large onions, chopped
¼ cup good-quality olive oil
2 zucchini, thinly sliced (or coarsely chopped broccoli, mushrooms, tomatoes, in
    any combination)
1 tablespoon dried basil (3 tablespoons fresh even better)
2 6-inch pitas, halved to form 4 rounds
¼ cup Parmesan cheese, grated
¼ pound mozzarella cheese, grated

Sauté onions in oil until soft and add sliced or chopped vegetables of your choice. Stir until vegetables are tender, about 5 minutes. Stir in basil and remove from heat.

Arrange pita rounds smooth side down on an ungreased baking sheet and sprinkle evenly with Parmesan cheese. Spread the vegetable mixture over the pitas and sprinkle with mozzarella.

Bake in the middle of a very hot oven—450 degrees—for 12–15 minutes or until cheese is bubbly and pita crust is golden brown and crisp. Serves 2–4.

Mixed Vegetable Casserole

4 medium carrots, sliced (about 2 cups)
12 ounces (or so) green beans, cleaned and cut into 1-inch pieces
2–3 cups cauliflower flowerets
1 onion, sliced
2 tablespoons butter
2 tablespoons flour
½ teaspoon salt
¼ teaspoon pepper
¼ cup dry sherry, if desired
½ cup heavy cream
½ cup grated Parmesan cheese

Preheat oven to 350 degrees. Simmer vegetables until crisp-tender. Drain and reserve liquid. Place vegetables in baking dish.

In a medium saucepan, heat butter until melted. Add flour, salt, and pepper and cook, stirring, until smooth. Add 1 cup reserved liquid and cream. Heat to boiling and add sherry, if desired. Cook for about 1 minute, stirring constantly. Pour sauce over vegetables and sprinkle with cheese. Bake for 20–30 minutes. Serves 6–8.

Layered Cheese and Vegetables

1 (10 ounce) package frozen broccoli spears or the equivalent fresh
1 package frozen lima beans
1 cup shredded Cheddar cheese
1 large onion, chopped
4 tablespoons margarine
2 teaspoons flour
1 (1 pound) can whole tomatoes, drained and chopped, and liquid reserved
Salt and pepper, to taste
Dried marjoram
1 cup soft bread crumbs
2 tablespoons grated Romano or Parmesan cheese

Cook broccoli and remove from cooking liquid with slotted spoon to a greased, shallow 2-quart baking dish. In the same liquid, cook lima beans, remove with slotted spoon and place over broccoli. Reserve liquid. Sprinkle Cheddar cheese over vegetables.

Sauté onion in 2 teaspoons margarine until soft. Sprinkle with flour and continue cooking, stirring, for about 2 minutes. Gradually add tomato liquid and cook gently, stirring, until smooth and thickened. Add chopped tomatoes and seasonings to taste. If sauce needs thinning, add some reserved vegetable liquid. Pour sauce over cheese and vegetables.

Sauté bread crumbs in remaining margarine until golden. Mix with Parmesan cheese and marjoram to taste and sprinkle over casserole. Bake in a 425-degree oven for 10–15 minutes or until topping is browned. Serves 4–6.

If you find yourself with tomatoes that are not as full flavored as you might wish, try sprinkling them with a pinch of sugar. It will enhance them enormously. This is particularly useful for those rather pale winter tomatoes, and while it won't turn winter into summer, it will help.

Eggplant, Tomato and Cheese Casserole

2 medium-sized eggplants, peeled and cut into ½-inch slices
¼ cup plus 2 tablespoons olive oil
2 onions, finely chopped
2 cloves garlic, mashed
2 zucchini, diced (about ¾ pound)
4 cups fresh ripe tomatoes, seeded and chopped
Black pepper
2 stalks celery, chopped
1 tablespoon chopped fresh basil or ½ teaspoon dried
⅓–½ cup grated Parmesan cheese
¼ cup chopped parsley
1½ cups small bread cubes made from crustless, firm bread
4 ounces or more part-skim shredded mozzarella cheese

Sprinkle eggplant slices with salt and let stand to drain for 15 minutes. Rinse off salt, dry thoroughly, and cut into ½-inch cubes.

Heat ¼ cup oil in a large skillet and sauté the eggplant quickly until it is lightly browned. Add onions, garlic, and zucchini. Cook several minutes more, adding oil if necessary.

Add tomatoes, pepper, celery, and basil. Bring to the boil and simmer covered for 15 minutes, or until zucchini is tender-crisp. Stir now and then.

Stir in the Parmesan and parsley and turn into two casserole dishes—one for now and one for the freezer.

Brown the bread cubes in remaining oil. Mix with mozzarella and sprinkle over casseroles. To serve place in 350-degree oven until cheese has melted.

Ratatouille

Makes lots and freezes well for summer flavors all winter.

2 cups good-quality olive oil
4 small eggplant (about 4 pounds) cut in 1½-inch cubes
2 teaspoons salt
5 onions, chopped
7 medium zucchini, quartered lengthwise and cut in 2-inch strips
2 medium green peppers, cut in ½-inch strips
2 medium sweet red peppers, cut in ½-inch strips
2 tablespoons minced garlic
3 cans (16 ounce) tomatoes, drained (or 5 cups fresh, chopped)
1 can (6 ounce) tomato paste
¼ cup chopped fresh dill
½ cup chopped fresh parsley
2 tablespoons dried basil or 4 tablespoons fresh
2 tablespoons dried oregano or 4 tablespoons fresh
Fresh ground pepper, to taste

Preheat oven to 400 degrees. Pour 1 cup olive oil into a large roasting pan. Add eggplant, sprinkle with salt, and toss. Cover with foil and bake about 35 minutes until eggplant is soft but not mushy. Uncover and let cool.

Heat remaining oil in a large skillet. Sauté onions, zucchini, peppers and garlic over medium heat for about 20 minutes. Add tomatoes, tomato paste, parsley, dill, basil, oregano, and pepper. Simmer 10 minutes, stirring now and then. Add eggplant and simmer another 10 minutes. Serves 12, hot or cold.

Ratatouille is great for end-of-summer garden bounty and very versatile. Proportions and seasonings can vary to suit your taste, it freezes beautifully, can be combined with meat and/or cheese to make a main dish, baked over fish fillets, can be a side dish, or served with small slices of good, dark bread with drinks before dinner.

Salads

Oriental Spinach Salad

6 cups spinach, cleaned, stemmed and torn into pieces
2 oranges, peeled and segmented—or 1 can mandarin oranges, drained
1 cup thinly sliced mushrooms
2–3 kiwi fruit, peeled and sliced
1 cup fresh mung bean sprouts, washed and dried
½ red onion, sliced thin and separated into rings
4 slices bacon, cooked and crumbled
1 cup toasted, slivered almonds

Dressing:

⅔ cup salad oil
¼ cup wine vinegar
2 teaspoons soy sauce
1 teaspoon sugar
1 teaspoon dry mustard
½–1 teaspoon curry powder
½ teaspoon garlic powder
¼ teaspoon ground pepper

Toss salad ingredients together. Combine dressing ingredients thoroughly and pour half on the salad. Toss until all spinach leaves are lightly coated. Save remaining dressing for another time. Serves 8.

Mushroom and Pepper Salad

1 large sweet red pepper
1 large sweet green pepper
¾ cup celery, cut into ¼-inch pieces
¼ pound mushrooms, sliced thin
2 unblemished endives
½ cup chopped scallions
2 tablespoons lemon juice
1 tablespoon red wine vinegar
3 tablespoons olive oil
¼ teaspoon sugar

Cut away the core end of the peppers and remove seeds and membranes. Bring some water to boil in a medium saucepan and cook pepper briefly—about 2 minutes. Remove peppers but save water.

Add celery to boiling water and simmer very briefly—about 30 seconds—and drain.

Cut peppers lengthwise into quarters, then cut the quarters crosswise into julienne strips ¼-inch thick.

Trim base of endives, then slice crosswise into pieces ¼-inch thick. Combine with all the vegetables in a salad bowl. In a small, screw-top jar place remaining ingredients, shake well, and toss with vegetables. Serves 4.

Holiday Green Salad

1 small head Boston lettuce
1 large or 2 small ripe pears
4 ounces Jarlsberg cheese, cubed
½ cup walnut halves
½ (4 ounce) package alfalfa sprouts
Mustard vinaigrette dressing (recipe below)

A few hours before serving wash and dry lettuce. Tear into bite-sized pieces. Place in plastic bag and chill. Chill pears. Remove cheese from refrigerator and allow to come to room temperature. Toast walnuts in a 350-degree oven for 10 minutes.

Shortly before serving, combine:

1 tablespoon white wine vinegar
3 tablespoons virgin olive oil
¼ teaspoon dry mustard
Salt and pepper to taste
Pinch of dried marjoram and ground cloves

To assemble salad, place lettuce and sprouts in large salad bowl. Slice pears thinly and add, along with cheese and walnuts. Drizzle on dressing, toss gently, and serve 4.

Fresh chopped fruit is often a good addition to salad. Some possible choices include unpared pears and apples, oranges and kiwi. Adds a touch of color and unexpected taste.

Hazelnut Salad from
The Silent Kitchen

For 40	*For 4*
100 cups hazelnuts (shelled, halved and blanched, if you wish)	10 cups
3 heads Romaine or spinach, bite-size	¼ head
3 heads Iceberg lettuce, bite-size	¼ head
10 oranges, peeled and cut, bite-sized	1
5 red onions, sliced thin	½
2½ cups sunflower oil	¼ cup
2½ cups red wine vinegar	¼ cup
¾ cup maple syrup	1 tablespoon
2½ teaspoons dry mustard	¼ teaspoon
5 cloves, halved garlic	½ clove
2½ teaspoons paprika	¼ teaspoon
2½ teaspoons salt	¼ teaspoon
½ teaspoon red pepper	pinch

Combine dressing ingredients at least 8 hours before serving.

To blanch hazelnuts place in a bowl, pour boiling water over, let stand 15 minutes, and slip skins off.

At serving time, mix salad ingredients and toss with dressing.

The Silent Kitchen

Throughout this book there are recipes from The Silent Kitchen which include amounts suitable for a crowd. The Episcopal Diocese of Vermont has its headquarters and conference center at Rock Point, an oasis of quiet natural beauty on the shore of Lake Champlain at the edge of Burlington, Vermont's largest city. Each year during Advent and Lent silent retreats are held there among the pines along the rocky shores, and for several years a group of friends calling themselves "The Silent Kitchen" came together to provide food for these weekends. They worked in silence to produce memorable meals, and their recipes are a very special legacy to all of us.

Celeste's Coleslaw from The Silent Kitchen

For 40	*For 4*
10 pounds cabbage, shredded	1½ pounds
2 cups onion, grated	½ cup
3 medium green peppers, minced	½ large
1½ cups maple syrup	⅔ cup
1½ cups salad oil	⅔ cup
1½ cups cider vinegar	⅔ cup
4 teaspoons celery seed	1 teaspoon
4 teaspoons salt	1 teaspoon

Mix together cabbage, onion, green pepper, and maple syrup. Boil together the oil, vinegar, celery seed, and salt. Let cool and mix into other ingredients.

This is best if made 12–24 hours before serving, and keeps for about 3 days.

Chimney Point

Day-Ahead Salad

This is a wonderful salad for entertaining as it can—indeed, must—be made the day before. The ingredients can be varied, and can include corn, red pepper, grated carrots, radishes, etc. Your eye for color is the determinant.

2–3 cups spinach, cleaned, stemmed and torn into pieces
1 teaspoon salt
¼ teaspoon fresh ground pepper
1 tablespoon sugar
1 pound bacon, fried and crumbled
4 hard-cooked eggs, sliced
2–3 cups shredded iceberg lettuce
1 (8 ounce) can water chestnuts, sliced
Salt, pepper, and sugar again as above
1 (10 ounce) package frozen peas, thawed
½ cup sliced Bermuda or green onions
1 cup mayonnaise
1 cup Miracle Whip
1 cup grated Swiss cheese

In a large, clear glass bowl, layer the ingredients in the order given, adding the salt, pepper and sugar after the spinach and again after the water chestnuts.

Mix mayonnaise and Miracle Whip and spread over the top of the salad, being careful to seal around the edge. Cover with grated cheese. Cover with plastic wrap and chill in the refrigerator overnight.

Lima Bean Salad

2 (10 ounce) packages frozen baby lima beans
4 tablespoons chopped parsley
1 clove garlic, minced
½ Spanish onion, chopped
¼ cup salad oil
2 tablespoons vinegar
Salt and pepper, to taste
3 tomatoes, peeled and sliced
½ Spanish onion, sliced thin and separated into rings

Cook beans according to package directions. Cool. Combine parsley, garlic, chopped onion, oil, vinegar, salt, and pepper and mix with cooled beans. Allow beans to marinate overnight in the refrigerator.

To serve, mound beans in center of platter and surround with sliced tomatoes and onion rings. Drizzle tomatoes and onions with more dressing if you wish. Serves 6.

An easy way to peel a clove of garlic is to smack it with the flat side of a large, heavy knife. The dry hull will separate easily. Another good smack with the knife will flatten the clove, allowing you to mince it quickly.

Broccoli Vinaigrette

A wonderful addition to the buffet table. May be prepared ahead.

1 (10 ounce) package frozen broccoli spears or equal amount fresh
4 tablespoons red wine vinegar
4 tablespoons salad oil
2 teaspoons minced parsley
4 teaspoons pickle relish
2 teaspoons minced chives
1 teaspoon minced capers
Salt and pepper, to taste

Cook broccoli until done but still crunchy. Drain and arrange in a serving dish.

Mix all remaining ingredients and pour over broccoli. Let stand for a bit to let flavors mingle. Serve either warm or chilled. Serves 4–6.

To reduce fat in oil-and-vinegar salad dressing use equal parts oil, vinegar, and water and intensify the flavor with fresh herbs and flavored mustard.

Crab Salad

2 pounds crabmeat, in bite-sized pieces
2 stalks celery, finely diced
1½ large red apples, cored and diced unpeeled
1½ tablespoons lemon juice, tossed with apple pieces
3 tablespoons fresh parsley, chopped
⅓ cup chopped chives or scallions
2 tablespoons finely cut dill weed
1½ cups mayonnaise

Combine all ingredients. Makes 2½ quarts.

Broccoli Salad

This salad is best made soon before serving as the broccoli tends to get soft—but you can prepare the parts ahead.

2 medium bunches fresh raw broccoli
1 medium onion, chopped
1 cup seedless raisins
1 cup mayonnaise
½ cup sugar
2 tablespoons vinegar
2 tablespoons milk
½ pound bacon, fried and crumbled

Wash broccoli, discard most of the stem, and cut heads into bite-sized flowerets. Put in a large mixing bowl along with onions and raisins. In a small bowl, mix mayonnaise, sugar, vinegar, and milk and pour over broccoli. Mix well. Sprinkle with bacon and chill a bit in the refrigerator. Serves 6.

Cauliflower Salad

1 head cauliflower, broken into bite-sized pieces
1 package (dry) garlic or herb salad dressing mix
⅔ cup salad oil
¼ teaspoon vinegar
2 tablespoons water
½ cup sour cream
½ cup bleu cheese
2 tablespoons crumbled cooked bacon
Slivered almonds

Steam cauliflower until tender-crisp. Mix remaining ingredients and blend well. Toss with cauliflower and chill. Serves 6.

Copper Carrots

2 pounds fresh carrots, sliced
2 medium onions, sliced thin
2 green peppers, cored and sliced thin
⅓ cup vegetable oil
¾ cup vinegar
1 cup sugar
1 (10 ounce) can tomato soup, undiluted
1 tablespoon prepared mustard
1 tablespoon Worcestershire sauce
Salt and pepper, to taste

Cook sliced carrots until they are still a bit crunchy. Drain and set aside.

In a medium saucepan mix the oil, vinegar, sugar, tomato soup, mustard, Worcestershire sauce, and seasonings. Bring to a boil and let cook for a minute.

Layer the vegetables in a bowl and pour sauce over them. Cover and let marinate in the refrigerator overnight. Will keep for about a month.

Vegetable Salad with Tuna Sauce

You can add things to your heart's content here. Potatoes and beans are the starting place, but the sauce compliments almost anything. Quantities depend on numbers of people, but the sauce as given dresses a salad for at least 12.

Red-skinned potatoes
Fresh green beans

Scrub potatoes well, but do not peel. Slice in ½-inch rounds and cook in lightly salted water until just tender. Drain potatoes well and let cool.

Wash beans and snip off stem ends. Steam until crisp-tender. Cool.

Meanwhile, prepare the sauce:

1 (6.5 ounce) can white tuna, drained
¼ cup fresh lemon juice
2 large egg yolks
¼ teaspoon cayenne pepper
½ teaspoon salt
4 cloves garlic, crushed
4 anchovies

Put everything in a blender and blend for a minute or two. While motor is running, add:

½ cup olive oil
½ cup vegetable oil

Arrange vegetables on a serving platter and drizzle sauce over them. Serve additional sauce on the side.

Cook leftover egg yolks in boiling water to hard boil for salads later.

Mixed Vegetable Salad

Another beautiful salad for your prettiest glass bowl. Choose a pleasing mixture of blanched and raw vegetables with enough variety of colors and consistency to make the final salad interesting. Some suggestions are:

Blanched vegetables:

Broccoli flowerets
Cauliflower
Carrot slices

Raw vegetables:

Mushrooms—firm and white
Sliced celery
Sliced zucchini
Sliced summer squash
Chopped red or green pepper (in moderation—these tend to take over)

Canned vegetables:

Corn, well drained
Artichoke hearts

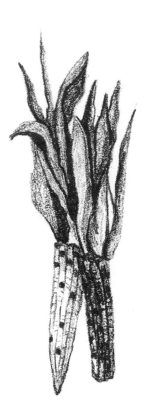

Blanch vegetables for a very short time (1–2 minutes) so as to intensify color but retain crisp texture. Immediately pour into a colander and run cold water over them until they are thoroughly cold to the touch. Drain completely on several changes of paper towels; this step is absolutely essential to the success of the dish.

Mix together the vegetables you have chosen and dress with one of the following: Mustard-mayonnaise (3 tablespoons brown mustard to 1 cup mayonnaise), French vinaigrette, or Italian dressing. Dress lightly and as close to serving time as possible. For a heartier salad, incorporate elbow macaroni or other small pasta into the vegetables, being sure to cook it *al dente* and dry thoroughly.

Jellied Beet Salad

1 package lemon gelatin—low calorie is fine
1 cup boiling water
1 teaspoon salt
2 tablespoons horseradish
2 tablespoons vinegar
1 tablespoon chopped onion
½ cup beet liquid
1½ cups diced (cooked or canned) beets

Mix gelatin and boiling water and stir until gelatin is dissolved. Add all other ingredients except beets and chill until slightly thickened. Fold in beets and spoon mixture into a well-rinsed and lightly oiled mold. Chill thoroughly. At serving time, turn out on chilled plate and serve with a sauce of equal parts mayonnaise and sour cream or plain yogurt. Serves 4.

Spinach Salad

Spinach, washed and torn in amount needed
¼ cup bleu cheese
½ cup sour cream
¼ cup mayonnaise
¼ cup yogurt
3 strips bacon, cooked crisp

Place spinach in salad bowl. Crumble bleu cheese over it. Combine sour cream, mayonnaise and yogurt and pour over all. Toss gently. Sprinkle with crumbled bacon.

Bean Salad

An old-time recipe with a difference—a good bet for a buffet or barbecue.

1 can green beans
1 can yellow beans
1 can kidney beans
1 can chick-peas
1 small can pitted black olives
1 small can pimentos, chopped
1 red onion, sliced
½ cup diced celery
½ cup diced green pepper

Drain canned vegetables and combine with remaining ingredients in a large bowl.

Make the following dressing:

1 cup vinegar
4 tablespoons salad oil
½ cup sugar
2 teaspoons nutmeg
½ teaspoon salt
¼ teaspoon grated pepper

Combine all ingredients and pour over vegetables, mixing well. Let sit in the refrigerator at least an hour, stirring occasionally. Serves 8.

Name _____

Address _____

City/State/Zip _____ Telephone _____

Please send me the best-selling classic cookbooks indicated below:

Title	Quantity	Price	Tax (Vermont residents only)	TOTAL
OUT OF VERMONT KITCHENS	_____	$12.95	$.65 per book	$ _____
VERMONT KITCHENS REVISITED	_____	$14.95	$.75 per book	$ _____
Total number of books ordered	_____	plus $2.00 each for shipping and handling		$ _____
			TOTAL ENCLOSED	$ _____

Since 1990   Since 1939

Please make checks payable to:
VERMONT KITCHEN PUBLICATIONS

Please do not send cash. Sorry, no C.O.D.'s.

Send to: Vermont Kitchen Publications
St. Paul's Cathedral
Two Cherry Street
Burlington, VT 05401
(802) 864-0471

Profits from the sale of these cookbooks are used to support the good works of St. Paul's Cathedral.
Prices subject to change without notice.

— —

Name _____

Address _____

City/State/Zip _____ Telephone _____

Please send me the best-selling classic cookbooks indicated below:

Title	Quantity	Price	Tax (Vermont residents only)	TOTAL
OUT OF VERMONT KITCHENS	_____	$12.95	$.65 per book	$ _____
VERMONT KITCHENS REVISITED	_____	$14.95	$.75 per book	$ _____
Total number of books ordered	_____	plus $2.00 each for shipping and handling		$ _____
			TOTAL ENCLOSED	$ _____

Since 1990   Since 1939

Please make checks payable to:
VERMONT KITCHEN PUBLICATIONS

Please do not send cash. Sorry, no C.O.D.'s.

Send to: Vermont Kitchen Publications
St. Paul's Cathedral
Two Cherry Street
Burlington, VT 05401
(802) 864-0471

Profits from the sale of these cookbooks are used to support the good works of St. Paul's Cathedral.
Prices subject to change without notice.

French Bean Salad

1 (1 pound) box dried small, white beans
1 onion stuck with 2 cloves
1 bay leaf
Salt and pepper
½ cup chopped scallions
½ cup minced parsley
½ cup vinaigrette dressing (of your choice)

Wash beans, cover with water to one inch above beans, and bring to a boil. Boil for 5 minutes. Turn off heat, let stand at least an hour. Drain, cover with cold water, add the onion, bay leaf, about 1 tablespoon salt, several grindings of pepper (or a couple of peppercorns) and simmer until beans are tender but not mushy. Check after ½ hour.

Drain, discard onion and bay leaf, and cool to room temperature. Carefully mix in scallions, parsley, and dressing. Serve at room temperature. Serves 4–6.

Mexican Salad

1 head lettuce, torn up
1 (15 ounce) can kidney beans, drained
½ onion, chopped
1 avocado, diced and sprinkled with lemon juice
4 ounces Cheddar cheese, shredded
½ bag tortilla chips, crumbled
1 red pepper, diced (optional)
French dressing (optional)

Put all ingredients in your prettiest salad bowl, toss everything together including dressing if you choose, and serve to 6–8 hungry eaters. (This salad works with or without dressing, so take your pick.)

Couscous Salad

(From the Church of Saint Luke in the Fields in New York City)

6 cups chicken stock
9 tablespoons olive oil
½ teaspoon ground ginger
½ teaspoon saffron
3 cups couscous
¾ cup currants
¾ cup dates, pitted and chopped
2¼ cups finely diced celery
1½ cups finely diced carrots
1 cup minced scallions
½ cup minced parsley
2¼ tablespoons freshly squeezed lemon juice
¾ teaspoon salt
½ teaspoon cinnamon
¾ cup walnuts

In a saucepan bring stock, ginger, saffron, and 6 tablespoons oil to a boil. Add couscous and boil until the liquid begins to be absorbed. Remove from heat and mix in currants and dates. Cover and let stand for 15 minutes. Add celery, carrots, and scallions. Mix well.

In a small bowl, combine parsley, lemon juice, salt, cinnamon, and remaining oil. Toss well with couscous, breaking up clumps. Cover and refrigerate overnight. Next day, bring to room temperature. Taste, adjust seasonings, and sprinkle with walnuts. Serves 16.

Wild Rice Salad with Currants and Pecans

1 cup uncooked wild rice
2¾ cups chicken stock
2¾ cups water
1 cup pecan pieces
1 cup currants
Grated rind of one orange
1 (10 ounce) package frozen tiny peas, thawed
¼ cup vegetable oil
⅓ cup fresh orange juice
1 teaspoon salt, or to taste
Freshly ground pepper, to taste

Rinse rice in strainer under cold running water. Combine with stock and water in pan. Bring to a boil, reduce heat and simmer, covered, 35–45 minutes, or until rice is *al dente*. Drain. Combine with remaining ingredients, mixing well. Let stand for about 2 hours before serving. Serves 6–8.

Wild Rice Arithmetic

1 pound wild rice measures 2⅔ to 2¾ cups
1 cup uncooked wild rice = 3 to 4 cups cooked
1 pound wild rice cooked = about 20 to 25 servings.

Herbed Potato Salad

2 pounds small, red-skinned potatoes
5–6 scallions, chopped
1 clove garlic, minced
2 tablespoons fresh chives, chopped
3 tablespoons parsley, chopped
1 tablespoon fresh tarragon, chopped (or 1 teaspoon dried)
¼ cup dry white wine
3 tablespoons oil
1 teaspoon red wine vinegar
Salt and pepper to taste

Boil potatoes in water to cover with a little salt until tender—15–20 minutes. Do not peel. Drain, cool, and slice ½-inch thick.

In a large bowl combine all remaining ingredients and mix well. Taste and adjust seasonings to your liking. Add sliced potatoes and gently combine. Serve warm or chilled. Serves 6–8.

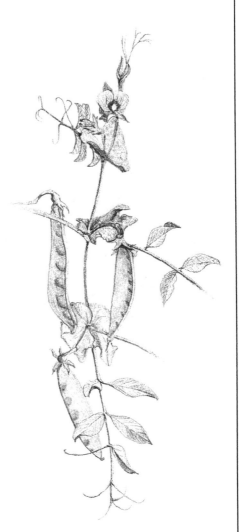

Red and Green Beef Salad

This is a pretty main-dish salad, especially nice in summer. Quantities are determined by the number of people you are serving: 1 pound of beef should serve 5. Use equal amounts of beef and vegetables.

Sirloin steak cooked to your liking and sliced very thin
Snowpeas, ends snipped, steamed for 1 minute
Cherry tomatoes, hulled

Grill or charbroil the beef, preferably medium rare. Toss beef and vegetables with the following dressing:

½ cup tamari
¼ cup sherry
7 cloves garlic, minced
1 tablespoon fresh ginger, minced
½ cup vegetable oil
1 tablespoon sesame seeds
¼ cup dry red wine

Process ingredients in blender 1 minute to make dressing.

Steak Salad

This is best served chilled on a warm day.

1¼–1½-pound boneless sirloin steak or fillet
¼ cup olive oil
1 red pepper, cut in strips
1 green pepper, cut in strips
1 yellow pepper, cut in strips
1 red onion, sliced thinly
1 tomato, cut in wedges, or cherry tomatoes
1 package tomatillos (Mexican green tomatoes)
1–2 tablespoons balsamic vinegar
¼ cup red wine vinegar
Basil, large pinch
Parsley, large pinch
Cilantro, if available, pinch
Salt and pepper, to taste

Cut steak into strips about ¼ inch thick, then sauté in hot olive oil until medium rare or to your taste. Remove from pan. Sauté peppers 1–2 minutes.

In a large bowl combine sliced red onion, tomatoes, tomatillos, vinegars, seasonings, and then add steak and peppers. Toss, serve, and enjoy. Serves 4.

Stroganoff Salad

A great buffet or summer dish.

3 pounds cooked roast beef or fillet of beef
Salt and freshly ground pepper to taste
1 cup mushrooms, sliced
2 tablespoons water
2 teaspoons lemon juice
2 Spanish onions
1 cup sour cream
2 teaspoons horseradish (or more for full flavor)
18 large ripe olives, sliced

Cut beef into ¼-inch julienne strips. Season well with salt and pepper. Place mushrooms in water and lemon juice and simmer, stirring, for about a minute. Drain and chill.

Combine beef with mushrooms, 1 chopped onion, sour cream and horseradish. Line serving dish with lettuce or any green leafy vegetable. Pile salad in middle and garnish with olives and onion rings from remaining onion.

If you only need 1 teaspoon of lemon or lime juice, roll the fruit on the counter to loosen the juice, then with a fork pierce a circle around the end opposite the stem end. Squeeze out what you need.

Smoked Turkey Salad

2 pounds smoked turkey, cubed (available at the deli counter of a good, big
    supermarket)
½ pound Jarlsberg cheese, julienned
2 cups green grapes, halved
2 cups red grapes, halved
1 cup sliced celery
1 cup cashews
1–2 bunches scallions, sliced (optional)
1½ cups mayonnaise
¼ cup dry sherry
2–4 tablespoons Dijon-style mustard

In a large bowl, combine turkey, cheese, grapes, celery, cashews, and onions
if you are using them. In a small bowl combine mayonnaise, sherry, and
mustard and mix well. Pour over salad and toss gently. Chill. Serves 10 as
a main dish.

Exotic Chicken Salad

1 small can pineapple, drained and juice saved
⅔ cup mayonnaise
1 tablespoon Dijon-style mustard
¾ teaspoon curry powder, or to taste
⅛ teaspoon salt
4 cups cooked chicken cubes
¼ cup chopped celery
2 tablespoons chopped onion
⅓ cup raisins
⅓ cup sliced or whole almonds

Combine pineapple juice with mayonnaise, mustard, curry powder, and salt. Taste and adjust seasonings.

Mix chicken with celery, onion, raisins, and almonds. Add dressing and combine well. Place in a lettuce-lined bowl, decorate with pineapple chunks (or green grapes) and serve to 6–8 as a main dish.

Chinese Chicken Salad

A wonderful dish for a potluck supper.

2 tablespoons soy sauce
1 tablespoon ground ginger
1 tablespoon dry mustard
6 tablespoons sugar
3 teaspoons salt—or to taste
1 ½ teaspoons black pepper
¾ cup salad oil
9 tablespoons red wine vinegar with garlic (or add a pressed clove)
2 pounds chicken breasts, baked and cubed
1 bunch scallions, chopped
1 (2 ¼ ounce) package blanched almonds, whole or sliced, toasted
8 tablespoons sesame seeds, toasted
½ package rice sticks, fried per package directions or chow mein noodles
1 medium head lettuce

Combine soy sauce, ginger, mustard, sugar, salt, pepper, oil, and vinegar and let stand for several hours.

Combine chicken, onions, almonds, sesame seeds, rice sticks or noodles, and lettuce. (Rice sticks can be found in the Chinese food section of your supermarket.)

Just before serving, toss with dressing. Serves 6–8.

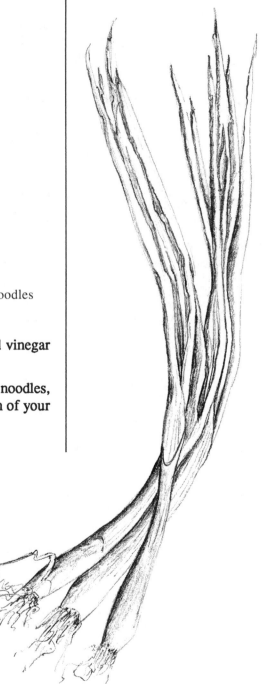

Wild Rice Salad
with Turkey and Ham

1 cup cooked wild rice
½ cup cooked white rice
8 scallions, chopped
½ pound fresh mushrooms, sliced
¾ pound cooked turkey or chicken breast, cubed
½ pound cooked ham, cubed
¾ pound seedless green grapes
1 cup slivered almonds

Mix all the above ingredients in a large bowl. Then toss gently with the following dressing:

3 tablespoons salad oil
2½ teaspoons prepared mustard
1¾ teaspoons sugar
¾ teaspoon thyme
⅓ teaspoon ground pepper

Just before serving, add 2 avocados, cubed. Serves 8 as a main dish.

Breads

Panton Vermont
Margaret Pardini

Sticky Buns

This recipe takes time to make but is well worth the effort. It is a famous and favorite treat around Middlebury and Burlington, wonderful for holiday breakfasts. Double the recipe at Thanksgiving, and freeze half for Christmas.

½ cup sugar
1½ teaspoons salt
½ cup margarine, softened
1 cup hot sieved or mashed potatoes (save cooking water)
1 package yeast
2 eggs
1½ cups warm potato water
7 cups flour, approximately
Walnuts, chopped (amount is up to you—1 cup+)
Brown sugar (amount indefinite)
Cinnamon-sugar mixture
Melted butter

Add sugar, salt, and margarine to hot potatoes. Cool to lukewarm and add yeast, eggs, and potato water. Mix well. Stir in flour to make a manageable dough.

Knead dough on floured surface until smooth. Place in greased bowl and let rise until double in bulk. Punch down and refrigerate until thoroughly chilled.

Butter 3 round or square cake pans. Cover bottoms with about ⅓ inch of brown sugar. Sprinkle on enough water to make sugar very wet, then sprinkle generously with chopped nuts.

Remove dough from refrigerator and roll out in a rectangle about ½ inch thick. Brush with melted butter and sprinkle with cinnamon-sugar mixture. Roll like a jelly roll and cut into ½-inch-thick circles. Place these side-by-side in prepared pans. Let rise until double.

Bake in a 350-degree oven 20–30 minutes. Immediately invert onto a plate while hot or buns will stick.

Nearly every 19th-century village had a grist mill where local grain became flour for homemade bread.

Puffy Breakfast Pancake

Easy, unusual, and delicious, especially served with jam or boiled cider. Try taking it to the table in the skillet and watch eyes pop!

6 tablespoons butter
½ cup flour
½ cup milk
2 eggs, lightly beaten
Pinch nutmeg
2 tablespoons powdered sugar
Juice of half a lemon

Preheat oven to 425 degrees. Use an oven-proof 12-inch skillet (or wrap the handle in aluminum foil to protect it). Add butter to skillet and melt in the oven as it heats.

In a bowl combine flour, milk, eggs and nutmeg. Beat lightly—leave a little lumpy. When skillet is very hot and butter melted, pour batter into the skillet and quickly return to the oven to bake for 15–20 minutes, or until golden brown.

Sprinkle with sugar and return briefly to oven—about 3–5 minutes. Sprinkle with lemon juice and serve, dividing into quarters for 4 large servings.

Sour Cream Pancakes

These pancakes are best made small and thin—about 3½ inches in diameter does it. Fan 4 of them attractively on each plate and serve with warm Vermont maple syrup, sliced firm McIntosh apples and good homestyle sausage. Guaranteed to take the chill off a fall or winter morning. Recipe can be halved easily.

4 eggs, separated
1 pint sour cream
4 tablespoons butter, melted
2 scant cups flour
1½ teaspoons baking powder
1 teaspoon salt

Beat egg yolks until thick. Add sour cream and melted butter. Combine well.

Mix dry ingredients together and stir into sour cream mixture.

Beat egg whites until stiff but not dry and fold into batter. (May be frozen at this point.) Thin with sweet or sour milk to make a batter which will produce pancakes of the thickness you desire—thinner may be poured onto hot griddle, thicker will have to be spooned on. Cook on each side until golden brown and serve immediately. Makes 45 3½-inch pancakes.

Cottage Cheese Pancakes

4 eggs
1 cup cottage cheese (low-fat is fine)
1 cup sour cream, sour milk, or low-fat yogurt
1 cup flour
1 tablespoon sugar

Put all ingredients in a food processor and blend briefly. Adjust the amount of milk or yogurt depending on the thickness of pancake you desire. Cook on a hot, greased griddle and serve with maple syrup, fruit syrup, boiled cider, or fresh fruit. Serves 4.

Sweet Potato Biscuits

1⅓ cups self-rising flour
2 teaspoons brown sugar
⅓ cup shortening
1 beaten egg
½ cup mashed, cooked sweet potato
2 tablespoons milk
Butter or margarine, melted

Preheat oven to 425 degrees. Stir together flour and brown sugar. Cut in shortening until mixture forms coarse crumbs. Beat together the egg, sweet potato, and milk, and add to dry mixture. Stir just until dough clings together. Turn out onto floured surface and knead 10 or 12 times. Roll ½-inch thick and cut with biscuit cutter or glass dipped in a little flour. Place on an ungreased baking sheet, brush with melted butter, and bake for 10–12 minutes.

Scones

2 cups flour
1 tablespoon baking powder
⅛ teaspoon salt
Scant ¼ cup sugar
4 tablespoons cold margarine or butter
¼ cup (or more) raisins or currants
2 eggs (or 1 whole egg and 2 egg whites)
¼ cup milk

Preheat oven to 375 degrees. Combine flour, baking powder, salt, and sugar in mixing bowl. Cut in butter or margarine with pastry blender, or by using pulse method in food processor, until crumbly. Add raisins or currants, lightly beaten eggs, and milk to make a soft dough. Add more milk if necessary. Place dough on well-floured surface, kneading to make smooth should dough require it, and divide in 2. Pat each piece into a ¼-inch thick circle and cut into 8 wedges. (16 in all.) Place wedges about 2 inches apart on ungreased baking sheet and bake for 15–20 minutes, or until golden brown.

For a shiny finish wedges may be brushed with an egg wash (1 egg beaten with a small amount of water) before baking.

Spiced Date-Nut Bread

1 teaspoon soda
1 cup boiling water
1 package dates, cut up
A piece of butter the size of a walnut (about 2 tablespoons)
1 cup sugar
1 egg, beaten
1½ cups flour
1 teaspoon each ground cloves and cinnamon
1 cup chopped walnuts
Grated rind of 1 lemon or orange

Combine boiling water with soda and pour over dates. Set aside.

Cream butter and sugar. Add eggs, dates and water. Then add flour, spices, nuts, and grated rind. Combine gently to mix. Pour into greased loaf pan and bake at 325 degrees for 1 hour.

Zucchini Bread

In late summer when gardens are producing more zucchinis than one can possibly use, consider grating some and freezing in 2-cup quantities for use during the winter.

¾ cup vegetable oil
½ cup white sugar
½ cup dark brown sugar
3 eggs, beaten
2 cups raw zucchini, grated
2 cups flour (can be half white and half dark)
½ teaspoon baking soda
3 teaspoons cinnamon
1 teaspoon baking powder
1 teaspoon salt
3 teaspoons vanilla
1 cup chopped nuts (or half nuts, half raisins)

Preheat oven to 300 degrees. Blend oil and sugar. Add beaten eggs and zucchini. Next add flour and remaining ingredients. Combine gently. Pour into 2 prepared loaf pans and bake for 1 hour.

You may divide batter into muffin pans. Bake at 350 degrees for 15–20 minutes. Will make 1½ dozen muffins.

To reduce fat in quick breads replace a half-cup of butter or oil with 3 ripe, very well-mashed bananas.

Glazed Lemon-Nut Bread

Bread:

6 tablespoons margarine, softened
½–¾ cup sugar, depending on your taste
2 eggs
Grated rind of 1 lemon
1½ cups flour
1 heaping teaspoon baking powder
½ teaspoon salt
½ cup milk
½ cup chopped nuts

Glaze:

Juice of 1 lemon
⅓ cup sugar

Grease and flour a loaf pan, and preheat oven to 350 degrees. Cream together margarine and sugar. Add eggs and lemon rind and mix well.

Sift together the flour, baking powder and salt. Add to creamed mixture alternately with the milk. Stir nuts in last and pour into prepared pan. Bake for 1 hour.

Remove bread to a rack to cool. Make a glaze by combining the lemon juice with ⅓ cup sugar, stirring to dissolve sugar. Pour this over the bread while it is still warm. You may wish to pierce the bread with a skewer in several places to allow glaze to penetrate the bread more fully.

Maple, Fruit, and Nut Bread

Boiling water
½ cup diced dried apricots
½ cup chopped dates
1 cup chopped nuts
3 cups flour
3 teaspoons baking powder
¼ teaspoon baking soda
1½ teaspoons salt
1 cup brown sugar
1 egg, lightly beaten
1 cup milk
½ cup maple syrup

Pour boiling water over apricots to cover and let stand for 15 minutes. Drain and mix with dates and nuts.

In a large bowl sift together flour, baking powder, baking soda, and salt. Add brown sugar and fruit/nut mixture. Mix well.

In a small bowl combine egg, milk, and syrup. Stir into dry ingredients until just mixed. Pour batter into 2 greased loaf pans, and let stand 15–20 minutes. Heat oven to 350 degrees and bake bread about 50 minutes. Cool before slicing—bread will slice better the second day.

Carrot, Fruit, and Nut Bread

2 cups flour
2 teaspoons soda
2 teaspoons cinnamon
½ teaspoon salt
1½ cups sugar
½ cup dried currants
½ cup flaked coconut
½ cup chopped pecans
1 cup vegetable oil
2 teaspoons vanilla
2 cups grated raw carrots
3 eggs

Preheat oven to 350 degrees. In a large bowl combine flour, soda, cinnamon, salt, and sugar. Add currants, coconut, and pecans. Then add oil, vanilla, carrots and eggs, mixing thoroughly. Pour batter into greased 9- x 5- x 3-inch loaf pan and let stand 20 minutes. Then bake about 1 hour. Cool slightly before removing from pan.

Keeps refrigerated up to 2 weeks and freezes well. Good served with cream cheese.

Vermont Apple Raisin Bread

For the best flavor, make your own applesauce from firm, flavorful autumn apples, and don't sweeten too much.

1½ cups unsifted flour
1 cup sugar
2 tablespoons cocoa
1 teaspoon soda
½ teaspoon salt
½ teaspoon cinnamon
½ teaspoon nutmeg
½ teaspoon allspice
½ cup buttermilk
1 cup applesauce
6 tablespoons melted butter or margarine
1 cup raisins
½ cup chopped walnuts
Powdered sugar

In a large bowl combine dry ingredients. In another bowl mix liquids together and stir into dry ingredients. Stir only until moistened. Add raisins and nuts and pour into a well-greased and floured 6-cup ring mold or bundt pan. Bake in a 325-degree oven for 45–50 minutes.

Cool bread in pan for 10 minutes, then turn out onto a rack. Sprinkle with powdered sugar. Serve plain or with cream cheese.

Oven Brown Bread

This recipe halves easily and exactly—but it also freezes beautifully, so why not make 2 to start with?

1 cup molasses
2 cups buttermilk or sour milk
2 teaspoons baking soda
1 cup white flour
2 cups dark flour
1 teaspoon salt
1 cup raisins (optional)

Preheat oven to 275 degrees. In a medium-size bowl combine the molasses, buttermilk, and soda, mixing with a wire whisk.

In a large bowl combine the remaining ingredients. Add liquids and beat well. Add raisins. Divide batter between 2 greased bread tins and bake for 1 hour. Makes 2 loaves.

Mixed Fruit Coffee Cake

1 (6 ounce) package dried fruit bits
⅔ cup brown sugar
1 tablespoon flour
1 tablespoon cinnamon
¾ cup shortening
¾ cup sugar
2 eggs
¾ cup milk
1 teaspoon vanilla
2 cups flour
2 teaspoons baking powder
½ teaspoon salt
5 tablespoons melted butter

Preheat oven to 350 degrees. Grease and flour a bundt pan or tube pan. Soak dried fruit in hot water to cover for 10 minutes. Drain.

In a small bowl, combine brown sugar, 1 tablespoon flour, 1 tablespoon cinnamon. In a large bowl, beat shortening with sugar. Beat in eggs, milk, vanilla. Combine remaining flour, baking powder and salt. At low speed beat in flour mixture to shortening mixture until just combined. Fold in dried fruit bits.

Spread ⅓ of batter evenly in bottom of prepared pan. Sprinkle with ⅓ of the cinnamon mixture, then drizzle ⅓ of the melted butter over that. Repeat layers 2 more times. Bake 55 minutes. Cool; remove from pan.

Poppy Popovers

2 eggs
1 cup milk
1 cup sifted flour
Dash of salt

Break the two eggs into a bowl. Add milk, flour, and salt. Mix with wooden spoon just until eggs are blended. Disregard lumps. Divide batter among 5 well-greased custard cups, or in a similarly prepared iron popover pan (this will yield more popovers).

Place in a *cold* oven. Turn on oven to 450 degrees and do not open oven door for ½ hour. Popovers should be tall and buttery-brown.

Puncture necks with a long-tined fork on 4 sides to let out steam. Return to oven for 10 minutes with heat off.

To reheat, place on cookie sheet without touching each other. Warm at 350 degrees for about 5 minutes.

Praline Muffins

These are exceedingly sweet little morsels. We recommend making them in the very small, 2½-inch party muffin tins and serving them in an assortment of breads for brunch.

2 eggs, lightly beaten
1 cup brown sugar
⅓ cup melted butter or margarine
½ cup *self-rising* flour
1 teaspoon vanilla
½ cup chopped pecans

Place paper liners in a muffin tin, if you are using them. Otherwise, butter the tin well. Fill them to ¾ full and bake in a 350-degree oven for 25 minutes. Makes 1 dozen 2-inch muffins.

Note: Small "party baking cups" can be found in many card and wrapping paper stores. Generally, they are less available in supermarkets.

Bran Refrigerator Muffins

A St. Paul's parishioner who runs a bed-and-breakfast says this is a great recipe—the best he's ever used.

1 (15 ounce) box raisin bran cereal
5 cups flour
3 cups sugar
5 teaspoons soda
2 teaspoons salt
1 cup nuts, chopped
1 cup raisins
4 eggs
1 cup salad oil
1 quart buttermilk

Mix dry ingredients, including nuts and raisins. In another bowl, beat eggs well and add oil and buttermilk to them.

Add liquids to dry ingredients, stirring just until all are blended together. Store in a tightly covered bowl. Will keep in the refrigerator 6 weeks.

To bake heat oven to 400 degrees, fill greased muffin tins ¾ full, and bake for 15–20 minutes. Makes 6 dozen large muffins, 12 dozen small ones.

Superior Spa Muffins

1½ cups whole wheat flour
½ cup oat or wheat bran
¾ teaspoon baking soda
¼ teaspoon freshly grated nutmeg
⅛ teaspoon ground cinnamon
2 teaspoons grated orange rind
½ cup peeled chopped apple
¼ cup raisins
¼ cup chopped walnuts
Juice of ½ orange
1 cup milk
1 egg, lightly beaten
¼ cup molasses
1 tablespoon oil

Preheat oven to 350 degrees. Lightly grease a 12-cup muffin pan. In a bowl, combine flour, bran, baking soda, nutmeg, and cinnamon. Stir in orange rind, apple, raisins, and nuts.

In another bowl, combine the remaining ingredients, then add them to the dry mixture. Stir quickly just until blended. Do not overmix. Fill muffin tins and bake for 25 minutes.

To make 1 cup of oat flour, blend 1¼ cups of rolled oats for 1 minute in a food processor or blender.

Oatmeal Muffins

1 cup rolled oats
1 cup buttermilk
1 egg
¼ cup brown sugar
⅓ cup vegetable oil
1 cup flour
1 teaspoon baking powder
½ teaspoon soda

Preheat oven to 400 degrees and lightly grease a 12-muffin tin. Combine rolled oats and buttermilk. Let stand 5–10 minutes. Then quickly combine with remaining ingredients, taking care not to overmix. Fill muffin tin ¾ full and bake for 15 minutes or until done. Makes 12 muffins.

Wheat Germ Muffins

1½ cups flour
1 cup wheat germ
1 teaspoon baking powder
½ teaspoon soda
¼ cup sugar
½ cup molasses
¼ cup vegetable oil
1 egg
⅔ cup milk

In one bowl combine dry ingredients. In another combine wet ingredients, and quickly combine the two. Take care not to overmix. Fill prepared muffin tins ¾ full and bake at 400 degrees for 10–15 minutes. Makes 12 muffins.

Cheddar Cheese Bread

6–7 cups unbleached white flour
1 tablespoon sugar
1 tablespoon salt
2 packages dry yeast
1½ cups water
¾ cup milk
2 tablespoons dried minced onion (or ½ small onion, minced)
3 cups sharp cheddar cheese, shredded

Preheat oven to 375 degrees and grease 2 loaf pans. In a large mixing bowl combine 3 cups flour, the sugar, salt, and undissolved yeast. In a saucepan heat water and milk to just below boiling, add onions, and set aside. When cool, blend into dry ingredients, mixing and beating well. Mix cheese with ½ cup of flour and add to dough, combining thoroughly.

Turn dough out onto floured surface and knead until smooth and elastic, working in just enough dough as you go along to control stickiness. Place in a buttered bowl, turning dough to coat evenly. Cover and let rise in a warm place until double in bulk.

Turn out on a floured surface, punch down, and knead lightly. Cover and let rest 20–30 minutes. Punch down again and divide in half, shape into loaves and place in prepared pans. Cover and let rise about 45 minutes, until doubled, and bake 45–60 minutes, until loaf makes a hollow sound when rapped. Turn out of pans and cool. Makes 2 loaves.

Quick French-Style Bread

1 package yeast
2 cups lukewarm water
1 teaspoon salt
1 tablespoon sugar
6 cups flour

Dissolve yeast in warm water. Add sugar and salt, stirring thoroughly. Add flour, 1 cup at a time, beating it in with a wooden spoon. Turn onto the counter, mixing in the last of the flour as you knead the dough for several minutes. When it is smooth, return it to a clean bowl, cover with a towel or plastic wrap, and set in warm place to double in bulk—about 1¼ hours.

Turn dough out on lightly floured surface, divide in 2, and shape into long or round loaves. Arrange on greased baking sheet. Allow to rise 5 minutes. Slash tops in 3 places with a sharp knife, brush with water, and put in a *cold* oven. Set oven temperature at 400 degrees, start it, and bake bread for 40 minutes. A pan of boiling water in bottom of oven makes crustier bread. Makes 2 loaves.

Cracked Wheat Bread

1½ cups boiling water
½ cup fine cracked wheat
¼ cup (4 tablespoons) butter or margarine, room temperature
1 tablespoon salt
4 tablespoons honey or maple syrup
1 package active dry yeast
⅓ cup warm water
1 cup warm milk
1 cup whole wheat flour
4 cups (more or less) white flour

In a large bowl pour boiling water over cracked wheat, margarine, salt, and sweetener. Stir to melt the margarine and let cool to lukewarm.

In a small bowl stir yeast into warm water and allow to proof. Add yeast along with milk to cracked wheat mixture.

Add flour, 1 cup at a time, until dough is stiff. Knead 8–10 minutes. When smooth and elastic form into a ball and place in an oiled bowl. Cover and let rise. Punch down and form into 2 loaves. Place in greased pans and let rise to tops of pans. Bake in a preheated 350-degree oven for 30–35 minutes. Cool on racks. Makes 2 loaves.

Tomato Herb Bread

1 tablespoon dry yeast
1 teaspoon sugar
2 tablespoons warm water
2¾ cups white flour
1 cup whole grain flour
2 tablespoons butter
2 tablespoons heavy cream
1 extra-large egg
1 (8 ounce) can tomato sauce
1 teaspoon dry basil or 2 tablespoons fresh, chopped
1 teaspoon dry parsley or 2 tablespoons fresh, chopped

Dissolve yeast and sugar in water. Process flour and butter in bowl of food processor, using metal blade, until just blended. Add all remaining ingredients to yeast mixture and stir. With processor running, pour this mixture through feed tube as fast as flour will accept the liquids. Process until dough cleans inside of bowl, adding flour by the tablespoon if dough is too moist, and cold water by the tablespoon if dough is too dry. Continue to process for about 40 seconds.

Turn onto a floured surface and knead a little bit. Place in an oiled bowl, turning to oil all sides of dough, cover, and set in a warm place until doubled in bulk—about 1½–2 hours.

Punch down dough, turn onto floured surface, and divide into thirds. Stretch each third into a long strip and connect the strips at one end. Braid strips together, stretching to make a loaf about 15 inches long. Tuck ends under and place loaf on a lightly greased baking sheet. Cover and allow to rise until double in bulk, about 45 minutes. Bake at 375 degrees for about 30 minutes, or until loaf is lightly browned and sounds hollow when rapped. Do not overbake. Cool on a wire rack. Makes 1 large, delicious loaf.

Oatmeal Bread

2 packages active dry yeast
½ cup warm water
2 cups rolled oats or a combination of rolled oats and oat bran
4 cups boiling water
1 tablespoon salt
¾ cup maple syrup
½ cup margarine
1 teaspoon instant coffee
1 cup whole wheat flour
4 cups, more or less, white flour

Stir yeast into warm water until dissolved and let stand until mixture is foamy.

Meanwhile, preheat oven to 350 degrees. Combine rolled oats (or combination), boiling water, salt, maple syrup, margarine, and instant coffee in a large bowl and cool to lukewarm.

Add yeast mixture to oat mixture and stir to combine. Add flour, 1 cup at a time, until dough is stiff. Turn out on a floured surface and knead for 8–10 minutes, or until dough is smooth and elastic. Cover and let rise in a warm place. Punch down, turn out on floured surface again, and knead lightly. Form 2 loaves and place in greased pans. Let rise to top of pans and then bake for 30–35 minutes—until loaves are golden brown and sound hollow when tapped. Cool on racks. Makes 2 loaves.

The best fiber sources are whole-grain flours; use them when you can. Substitute oat flour or oat bran for up to ⅓ of the flour in baked goods.

Herb and Onion Bread—
a batter yeast bread

½ cup milk
1½ tablespoons sugar
1½ teaspoons salt
1 tablespoon butter
1 package dry yeast
½ cup warm water
2¼ cups white flour, or a combination of white and whole wheat flour
½ small onion, chopped
½ teaspoon fresh dill
1 teaspoon crushed, dried rosemary

Preheat oven to 350 degrees. Scald milk and dissolve in it the sugar, salt, and butter. Cool to lukewarm.

In a large bowl dissolve yeast in warm water. Add cooled milk mixture, flour, onion, and herbs. Stir well with a wooden spoon. Set in a warm place, covered, and let rise until triple in bulk—about 45 minutes.

Stir down dough and beat vigorously for a few minutes. Turn into a greased 8- x 4-inch bread pan and let stand in a warm place for about 10 minutes. Then place in preheated oven and bake about 1 hour. Makes 1 loaf.

The dough can be baked in muffin tins for 30 minutes, if you prefer.

Dill Bread

The fresh dill adds both color and flavor. If you use a food processor and add it during the first mixing stage, it will come out as little specks through the loaf. If you prefer the idea of little sprigs of dill, coarsely chop about eight stems of the fresh herb and incorporate during the kneading.

2 cups low-fat cottage cheese
2 tablespoons butter or margarine
1 tablespoon dill seed
Fresh dill to your taste
2–3 tablespoons minced chives
¼ cup honey
¼ teaspoon baking soda
1 teaspoon salt
2 eggs, beaten
1 package dry yeast dissolved in ½ cup warm water
5–6 cups unbleached flour

Slightly warm the cottage cheese and butter. Add dill seed, chives, honey, baking soda, salt, dill, and eggs. Beat until blended. If you use a food processor or heavy-duty mixer, you can just drop the eggs in unbeaten. Add yeast mixture and beat some more. Start adding flour until your particular appliance says "quit," and then turn the dough out onto a well-floured surface and knead until smooth, adding flour as needed. Place in an oiled bowl, turning to coat thoroughly, cover with a damp towel, and set in a warm, draft-free spot until doubled in bulk, about an hour. Then turn onto kneading surface and knead lightly for a few minutes.

Cover and let rest while you oil the bread pans and pre-heat the oven to 375 degrees. Form dough into loaves (2 big ones, 3 small ones), place in prepared pans, cover and let rise until dough reaches tops of pans. Bake for about 35 minutes or until nicely browned and hollow-sounding when tapped on the bottom. Remove from pans immediately and let cool on racks before slicing. Makes 2 large or 3 small loaves.

Cheese Rolls from The Silent Kitchen

16 dozen	*4 dozen*
4 cups water	1 cup
2 cups rolled oats	½ cup
8 tablespoons butter	2 tablespoons
1 ½ quarts milk	1½ cups
8 tablespoons maple syrup	2 tablespoons
8 tablespoons dry yeast	2 tablespoons
8 cups whole wheat flour	2 cups
2 cups potato or gluten flour	½ cup
8 tablespoons salt	2 teaspoons
8 eggs	1
6 cups Cheddar cheese, shredded	1½ cups
16 cups white flour	4 cups

Heat water to boiling and pour over rolled oats and butter. Let cool to lukewarm. Meanwhile, heat milk until it feels very warm on the wrist, add maple syrup, and sprinkle on the yeast. Let stand 10 minutes in a warm place.

When yeast has proofed, add oat mixture, whole wheat flour, potato flour, salt, eggs, and cheese. Beat well. Mix in white flour, 1 cup at a time, until dough leaves sides of bowl but is not too stiff. Turn onto lightly floured board and knead for 10 minutes. Place in oiled bowl, turning to grease all sides, cover, and let sit in a warm place for about 45 minutes, or until doubled in bulk. Punch down and roll out to ½-inch thickness on floured board and cut with scissors into strips ½ inch x 3 inches. Roll strips into cylinders and tie into single or double knots. Place on greased cookie sheets; let rise about 30 minutes and bake in a 400-degree oven for 15–20 minutes.

To keep rolls warm at the table, heat a ceramic tile in the oven, put under rolls in bottom of bread basket, cover with napkin, and all will stay warm during the meal.

Sweets

Larrabee's Point

McIntosh Cake

Good anytime, but especially in the fall, when apples are newly harvested, fresh and firm.

1½ cups sugar
1 cup vegetable oil
2 teaspoons vanilla
4 large eggs
¼ cup unsweetened apple juice
3 cups unbleached flour
¾ teaspoon salt
2 teaspoons baking soda
1 tablespoon cinnamon
4 medium McIntosh apples, cored and sliced, but not peeled

Combine sugar, oil, and vanilla in mixer bowl and beat at medium speed until thick, about 3 minutes. Add eggs and apple juice, and beat at high speed until thick and lemon-colored, about 3 more minutes. Add dry ingredients and beat on low until combined. Batter will be very thick.

Add sliced apples. Beat on low speed for a few seconds, just long enough to break up apples but not reducing them to a pulp. Spoon batter into a 10-inch tube pan heavily greased with solid shortening, not oil.

Bake at 325 degrees for 1 hour and 25 minutes, or until tester comes out clean. Cool in pan 30–45 minutes, then remove and cool completely.

Applesauce Cupcakes

Nutritious and sugar free!

1 cup unbleached flour (or ½ cup unbleached and ½ cup whole wheat)
½ teaspoon cinnamon
¼ teaspoon each nutmeg, ginger, cloves, salt, and soda
2 teaspoons granular sugar substitute
1 egg
1 teaspoon vanilla
¼ cup butter or margarine, melted
½ cup unsweetened applesauce

Preheat oven to 350 degrees and prepare a muffin tin by greasing or inserting cupcake papers.

Mix together the dry ingredients. In a separate bowl stir together the egg, vanilla, melted shortening, and the applesauce. Combine with dry ingredients, stirring only enough to moisten. Divide batter into prepared muffin tin and bake 20–25 minutes.

Apricot Upside-Down Cake

The topping (or the "bottoming," if you please)

⅔ stick butter
1 cup light brown sugar
1 can unpeeled apricot halves

Melt butter in a 9- or 10-inch iron frying pan, spread sugar evenly over the bottom and remove from heat. Cover sugar with apricot halves, cut side up, allowing a little bit of juice to drizzle in. Set aside and heat oven to 350 degrees.

The cake:

1½ cups sifted cake flour
1½ teaspoons baking powder
⅛ teaspoon salt
⅔ cup sugar
⅓ cup shortening
1 egg
½ teaspoon vanilla
½ cup milk

Sift together flour, baking powder, and salt. Beat together sugar, shortening, egg, and vanilla. Add flour and milk alternately to well-beaten sugar-shortening mixture. Spoon batter evenly over apricots and bake 40–50 minutes until cake is light brown and pulls away from sides of pan. Let rest 10 minutes before inverting onto a large plate. Scrape any remaining topping onto cake. Lemon sauce is a nice complement. Serves 6–8.

Pineapple Cake with Ginger Frosting

2 eggs
1 (20 ounce) can crushed pineapple
2 cups flour
1 cup granulated sugar
1 cup brown sugar
2 teaspoons baking soda
1 cup chopped walnuts

Preheat oven to 350 degrees. In a large mixing bowl, beat eggs until light and fluffy. Add pineapple, including juice. Add flour, sugars, and baking soda. Mix well. Then stir in walnuts and spread batter evenly in ungreased 9- x 13-inch pan. Bake for 40–50 minutes or until tester comes out clean. When cake cools, frost.

Frosting:

3 ounces cream cheese
¼ cup butter, softened
1 teaspoon vanilla
2 cups powdered sugar
½ teaspoon ginger
1 teaspoon grated lemon rind

In a small bowl, beat cream cheese, butter, and vanilla until smooth. Gradually add sugar, ginger, and lemon peel. Beat until smooth and frost cooled cake. Sprinkle with additional chopped nuts if you wish.

Lemon-Nut Pound Cake

This keeps well, and is good by itself or as a base for berries or chocolate sauce.

2 sticks butter or margarine at room temperature
1 cup sugar
4 eggs at room temperature
1 tablespoon grated lemon peel (about 2 lemons' worth)
2½ cups unbleached flour
½ teaspoon salt
1 teaspoon baking powder
1 teaspoon baking soda
1 cup yogurt at room temperature
¾ cup finely ground nuts—pecans or almonds are good

Glaze:

½ cup lemon juice
½ cup sugar

Preheat oven to 350 degrees and thoroughly grease a 9-inch tube pan or bundt pan.

Cream softened butter and sugar together until light and fluffy. Add eggs and lemon peel, blending well.

Sift dry ingredients together and add alternately with yogurt to butter mixture. Fold in ground nuts. Turn into prepared pan and bake about 1 hour, or until tester comes out clean.

While cake is still warm, combine lemon juice with ½ cup sugar in a saucepan and heat until sugar dissolves. Pour slowly over cake. Allow to cool in pan.

Put lemons in hot water before squeezing and they will give you twice as much juice. Zap for 10–15 seconds in the microwave for same result.

Orange Chocolate Cake

Read this one all the way through before beginning. It is easier than you might think, but does require some organizing.

1½ ounces baking chocolate, melted
2 eggs, separated, with each white kept separate
½ cup shortening
1½ cups sugar
Grated rind of ½ orange
2½ cups flour
¼ teaspoon salt
4 teaspoons baking powder
1 cup milk

Preheat oven to 350 degrees and grease two 8- or 9-inch cake pans. Beat one egg white until stiff but not dry and set aside.

Cream shortening with sugar until fluffy and add orange rind. Next add egg yolks which have been lightly beaten. Sift together the flour, salt, and baking powder and add alternately with the milk. Fold in beaten egg white.

Divide batter into 2 parts. To one part, add melted chocolate, blending thoroughly. Spoon batter into prepared cake pans, alternating spoonfuls of light and dark. Bake 25–30 minutes. Cool for 5 minutes, then turn out of pans. When thoroughly cool, frost as follows:

Frosting:

3 tablespoons butter, melted
3 cups powdered sugar
Grated rind of ½ orange
2 tablespoons orange juice
Pulp from 1 orange, with seeds and membranes removed
1 egg white, beaten until stiff
2½ ounces baking chocolate, melted

Combine butter, sugar, orange rind, and orange juice, stirring until smooth. Stir in pulp, and fold in beaten egg white. Frosting will be thick and fluffy.

The best cakes and pies win blue ribbons at end-of-summer fairs and agricultural field days where baking talent is judged as important as raising tomatoes or sheep.

Choose one cooled layer to be the top of your cake, and spread orange frosting on its top. While it is soft, dribble some melted chocolate on it in a sort of marble pattern.

To the rest of the orange frosting, add the rest of the melted chocolate, mixing well. Spread this chocolate-orange frosting over second cake layer, and carefully place orange-frosted layer on top of it. Then frost sides of assembled cake with remainder of chocolate frosting. Delicious!

Old-Time Fudge Cake

⅔ cup soft shortening (part butter, part margarine)
1¾ cups sugar
2 eggs
1 teaspoon vanilla
2½ ounces baking chocolate, melted
2½ cups sifted cake flour, or 2¼ cups all-purpose flour
1½ teaspoons soda
½ teaspoon salt
1½ cups ice water

Preheat oven to 350 degrees. Grease 2 8-inch layers or 1 9- x 13-inch pan.

Cream together shortening and sugar. Add eggs and vanilla and continue beating until light and fluffy. Beat 5 minutes. Blend in cooled chocolate. Sift together flour, soda, and salt. Add to creamed mixture alternately with ice water. Bake in prepared pan(s) for 30–35 minutes. A dense, rich cake.

¼ cup cocoa and 2 teaspoons oil = 1 ounce baking chocolate.

Mother's Gingerbread

Wonderful served with hot applesauce—or for a different taste treat, try hot lemon sauce.

1½ cups flour
½ cup molasses
½ cup shortening, melted
½ cup hot water
½ cup sugar
1 teaspoon ground ginger
½ teaspoon ground cinnamon
1 teaspoon soda
A pinch of salt
1 egg

Preheat oven to 350 degrees. Grease a 7- x 12-inch or 9- x 9-inch pan. Mix all ingredients together without beating egg first. Pour into prepared pan and bake for 30 minutes, or until tester comes out clean.

To sour milk: bring a cup of milk to room temperature, add a tablespoon of lemon juice or white vinegar, and let stand for 10–15 minutes, until milk begins to thicken.

Frozen Lemon Pie

3 eggs
1 cup sugar
½ cup lemon juice
Grated rind of 1 lemon
1 cup heavy cream, whipped
Graham cracker crumbs to make generous layer in 9- or 10-inch pie plate

Beat eggs and add sugar. Cook, either in double boiler or over direct heat, while stirring until mixture thickens. Stir in lemon juice and lemon rind. Cool.

Fold in whipped cream and pour over crumbs. Sprinkle with more crumbs and freeze until serving time. Serves 8.

Beggar's Cake

3 cups all-purpose flour
2 teaspoons soda
1 teaspoon cinnamon, or a mixture of any sweet spices
 like nutmeg, mace, cloves
½ teaspoon salt
2 cups sugar
1½ cups oil
1 teaspoon vanilla
½ teaspoon lemon extract
1 cup crushed pineapple with juice
2 cups finely grated carrots, or a mixture of carrots, sweet potato,
 chopped nuts, raisins
3 eggs

Preheat oven to 350 degrees. Grease a 10- x 15-inch flat baking pan. Mix flour, soda, spices, and salt. Combine sugar, oil, vanilla, and lemon extract. Add to dry ingredients. Add pineapple, carrots, etc., and mix everything well. Add eggs and mix again. Pour into prepared pan and bake for about 1 hour and 15 minutes, or until tester comes out clean.

Mashed banana may be substituted for the pineapple. Serve dusted with powdered sugar or frosted with a not-too-sweet cream cheese icing.

In baking, recipes requiring 1 or 2 eggs may usually be altered satisfactorily by substituting 2 egg whites for 1 whole egg, thereby eliminating cholesterol.

Boiled Maple Cake

1 cup maple syrup
½ cup shortening, melted
1 teaspoon each cloves, nutmeg, cinnamon, and salt
1 cup seedless raisins
1 cup cold water
2 cups flour
1 teaspoon soda
½ cup chopped nuts

Grease and flour a loaf pan. Preheat oven to 350 degrees. In a saucepan combine syrup, shortening, spices, salt, raisins, and water. Boil together for 4 minutes, then chill thoroughly.

Add flour, soda, and nuts, beating well. Pour into prepared loaf pan and bake for 1 hour, or until tester comes out clean.

For added richness, frost with a maple frosting and sprinkle with chopped nuts.

For an easy maple frosting: Beat 2 egg whites until stiff but not dry, then boil ¾ cup maple syrup and ¼ teaspoon cream of tartar to the soft-ball stage. Quickly remove from heat and gradually pour the syrup over the egg whites as you beat everything together with an electric mixer until it is light and spreadable.

Pumpkin Cheesecake

Crust:

¾ cup graham cracker crumbs
2 tablespoons sugar
2 tablespoons melted butter

Preheat oven to 350 degrees. Mix ingredients for crust and pack into bottom of 9- or 10-inch spring-form pan.

Filling:

1 pound cream cheese, softened
⅔ cup white sugar
⅔ cup brown sugar, packed
¾ cup heavy cream
6 eggs, lightly beaten
1 teaspoon cinnamon
⅓ teaspoon grated nutmeg
1⅓ cups canned, unspiced pumpkin

Beat cheese and sugars together. Add lightly beaten eggs and mix well. Add cream and beat until smooth and light. Add spices and pumpkin, and again, beat until smooth and light. Pour into spring-form pan over crust. Place in a pan of water and bake in preheated oven for 1 hour. Turn oven off and let cake remain in oven for another hour.

Topping:

1 cup chopped nuts
⅔ cup brown sugar, packed
2 tablespoons butter, melted

Mix ingredients together and sprinkle over top of pie about 10 minutes before it finishes baking. This is a large cheesecake and will serve lots, depending on size of slices.

A crisp lettuce leaf in a container of hard brown sugar will soften it up. Sounds like magic but it works.

Thanksgiving Pumpkin Pie

Fresh pumpkin and maple syrup seal Vermont into this pie.

2 small pumpkins
4 eggs
1 cup maple syrup
1 cup cream
2 tablespoons molasses
2 teaspoons vanilla
¼ teaspoon salt
2 teaspoons cinnamon
1 teaspoon ginger
½ teaspoon cloves
½ teaspoon allspice
¼ teaspoon grated nutmeg
1 unbaked 10-inch pie shell

Buy the pumpkins before Halloween, draw faces on them for the festivities, and next day bring them inside. Cut in half, scoop out the seeds, and put them face down on a baking sheet covered with ¼ inch water. Bake at 350 degrees 1 hour or until soft. Spoon out pulp, measure 3 cups, and freeze for Thanksgiving. Use remaining pulp for another pie.

To make the pie, thaw the pulp, and purée it with all the other ingredients in a blender or food processor. Pour into an unbaked crust in a 10-inch pie pan. Bake at 450 degrees for 10 minutes, then reduce heat to 350 degrees and bake 45 minutes more or until set. Serves 8–10.

Cool before cutting, and serve with whipped cream if desired. And be thankful.

When the fall hillsides turn a glorious gold and scarlet many towns celebrate with festivals. These often feature suppers or pie sales where the pies of choice are pumpkin and apple, fall flavors in a crust.

Maple Syrup Pie

An old-fashioned Vermont pie—quite sweet, so a little goes a good way.

1½ cups maple syrup
½ cup water
½ cup flour
Pinch of salt
2 tablespoons butter
3 eggs, separated
¼ cup cream
1 baked pie shell

Combine maple syrup and water. Whisk in flour and salt, and continue whisking while bringing to a boil. Whisk and boil for a minute or so.

Add butter. When butter is melted, add about ½ cup of hot syrup mixture to 3 egg yolks, beating all the while. Then whisk egg yolk mix back into syrup mix, add cream, and continue to cook and stir until filling thickens—4 or 5 minutes.

Pour into pie shell and cover with meringue made from 3 egg whites and 6 tablespoons sugar. Spread over maple filling and bake at 425 degrees for about 5 minutes, or until meringue is light brown.

Variations: Add ½ to 1 teaspoon rum extract to filling or ¾ cup chopped walnuts.

Sugar maples love Vermont and more grow here than any other place, thriving on its rugged soil and climate. The state leads the country in maple syrup production. The working life of a sugar maple begins at 40 when it is ready to be tapped. In late winter as days warm but nights remain cold, 4 maple trees will yield the 35–40 gallons of sweet, waterlike sap needed to boil down to 1 gallon of maple syrup.

Pure Vermont syrup is nothing like the so-called maple syrup in the super-market which is mostly corn syrup and coloring. The real thing is saturated with flavor, expensive, and worth every penny.

Fresh Orange Pie

Over 100 years old, this wonderful recipe comes to us from the Nebraska memories of a present-day Vermont cook.

1 baked pie shell
1½ cups sugar
⅓ cup flour
2 tablespoons cornstarch
Pinch of salt
3 eggs, separated
Grated rind of 1 orange
1 tablespoon lemon juice
Juice of ½ orange
1⅓ cups boiling water
1 teaspoon butter

Mix sugar, flour, cornstarch, and salt. In a small bowl beat egg yolks, and add sugar-flour mixture to them. Mix in orange rind and the juices.

In a saucepan bring water to a boil, then add above mixture to it, stirring constantly. When well combined, place pan over more boiling water (in a double boiler) and cook until thickened, stirring. Cook for 10 minutes after it thickens. Cool and pour into baked pie shell.

Meringue:

3 egg whites
1 tablespoon orange juice
1 tablespoon lemon juice
¼ teaspoon cream of tartar
6 tablespoons sugar
Pinch of salt

Beat egg whites, juices, and cream of tartar for 3 minutes at high speed, until they start to become firm. Add sugar gradually while continuing to beat, then salt. Beat until meringue is glossy and holds its shape. Spread over orange mixture and bake in a 300-degree oven for about 25 minutes.

Gaga's Lemon Pie

8-inch cooked pie shell

Filling:

4 egg yolks
1 cup sugar
½ cup lemon juice
1 egg white
Pinch of salt
Grated rind of 1 lemon

Beat egg yolks in mixer until very light and fluffy. Add sugar slowly while beating. Then add juice, beating. Add unbeaten egg white, still beating. Stir in salt and lemon rind. Pour into top of double boiler over hot water and cook, stirring constantly, until mixture thickens and coats a spoon. Take off the simmering water and cool. Pour into pie shell.

Meringue:

3 egg whites
¼ teaspoon cream of tartar
6 tablespoons sugar
¾ teaspoon vanilla

Turn oven on to 300 degrees. Add cream of tartar to egg whites and beat until stiff. Sprinkle sugar in very slowly while beating; then add vanilla. Egg whites should be thick and glossy. Spread over lemon filling, being sure to seal against the crust. Bake for 15–20 minutes. Turn oven off and leave pie in until cool.

Grape Pie

A wonderful way to take advantage of fall's bountiful crop of Concord grapes.

9-inch unbaked pie shell
3½ cups Concord grapes
1 cup sugar
¼ cup flour
¼ teaspoon salt
1 tablespoon lemon juice
1½ tablespoons butter

Slip skins from grapes (not hard; try it!) and set skins aside. Boil grape pulp a few minutes, then press through a sieve to remove seeds. Return skins to pulp.

Combine sugar, flour, and salt, then add, along with lemon juice and butter, to grape pulp. Mix well. Pour into prepared pie shell and sprinkle with the following topping:

¾ cup flour
½ cup sugar
⅓ cup butter

Combine flour and sugar; cut in butter until crumbly. Sprinkle evenly over pie and bake at 400 degrees for 45–50 minutes.

Apple Cream Pie

From a Vermont great-grandmother, concocted in "olden times" when mid-winter stores were low and the cold cellar yielded little for dessert save the remains of the fall apple crop.

Pie crust sufficient for one 10-inch pie
1 cup "top milk" (half and half)
½ cup sugar
2 tablespoons flour
5 cups peeled, sliced apples

Set oven at 450 degrees. Mix flour with sugar. Mix in the cream and combine well. Arrange apple slices in the prepared pie plate and pour cream mixture over all. (No top crust) Bake at 450 degrees for 10 minutes, then reduce oven to 350 degrees and continue baking another 45 minutes.

Old-Fashioned Peach Pie

1 recipe pastry for a 9-inch, 2-crust pie
¾ cup sugar
3 tablespoons flour
½ teaspoon nutmeg or cinnamon
5 cups sliced peaches
2 tablespoons butter or margarine

Combine sugar, flour and spices. Add to peaches and mix lightly. Spread in 9-inch pastry-lined pie plate. Dot with butter. Top with lattice strips and bake at 400 degrees for about 45 minutes.

This pie may be varied by adding a cup or so of fresh blueberries to the peaches.

To make your own crème fraîche, thoroughly combine 1 tablespoon buttermilk or sour cream with 1 cup heavy cream. Set aside, covered loosely, 24 to 48 hours until thick. Covered tightly, it can then be refrigerated for at least a week. It is delicious on fresh strawberries and desserts, or use as the French do to thicken sauces.

Mile-High Strawberry Pie

9-inch baked pie shell
1 (10 ounce) package frozen strawberries, thawed until mushy
½ cup granulated sugar
Dash of salt
2 unbeaten egg whites
1 teaspoon lemon juice
½ cup heavy cream
½ teaspoon vanilla

In a cold bowl with a cold beater beat strawberries, sugar, salt, egg whites, and lemon juice for 15 minutes.

Whip cream until thick, add vanilla, and fold into strawberry mixture. Pour into pie shell and place in freezer until serving time. Keep frozen at all times! Serves 8.

PANTON TOWN HALL, PANTON, VT.
BUILT AS METHODIST CHURCH – 1835

Never-Fail, Freeze-Ahead Pie Crust

5 cups flour
2½ cups shortening
3 teaspoons baking powder
1½ teaspoons salt
1 egg
2 teaspoons vinegar

Work together the flour, shortening, baking powder, and salt, cutting together with pastry blender or knives. Break egg in a 1-cup measure, add vinegar, and fill cup with water. Add to flour mixture and blend everything together. Mixture will be moist.

Put bowl in refrigerator for several hours. Then divide dough into balls equal to size of one pie crust. Place in plastic bags and freeze. Thaw what you need when you need it. This makes 3 or 4 double-crust pies.

Maple Sugar-on-Snow

Reflections from a Vermont farm girl who grew up . . . .

Sugaring season is a special time on the farm. It heralds spring. It's the time when days are warmed by the sun, but nights are still winter, and the roads turn to mud. It's the time when we start eyeing the snow drifts to see which ones will give us a supply of good, clean snow for sugar-on-snow. Clean snow may indeed be the most difficult thing for city dwellers to find if they set their hearts on having this candy-like treat.

Most Vermonters know how to make sugar-on-snow: "You pour some maple syrup in a pot and boil it until it's done." But that's not much help, is it? We'll try to take it step-by-step.

Send some reliable children out to gather large pans full of *clean* snow, well packed. You will want one pan for every two people. Have them also bring in a small pan of snow to use for testing.

Rub the rim of a 6-quart pot with butter to prevent a "boiling over." Pour about a quart of good maple syrup into the pot. Bring to a simmer over low heat, and the evaporation process begins. The idea is to make the syrup dense enough to lay on top of the snow. When it begins to thicken, test it regularly by dropping a teaspoonful on the testing snow.

When it sits there in a little golden disk that droops when you pick it up with a fork, it's done. Take it off the heat *immediately*. Pour the hot syrup into little pitchers, and pass it to be drizzled over the snow. There are several schools of thought as to how this should be done. We prefer little puddles about the size of a half-dollar. Others like great, long spirals that wind around the fork. In any form it is delicious!

We always served it with hard-boiled eggs, sour dill pickles, and homemade, plain raised doughnuts.

Two Easy, Very Vermont Desserts

Maple Custard

Put 4 eggs into the blender. Add milk to make 1 quart. Add maple syrup to taste, and blend briefly. Pour into custard cups and place in pan of water. Dust with nutmeg. Bake at 325 degrees until knife comes out clean, about 45 minutes or so.

Maple Apples

Quarter and core however many firm, flavorful apples you will need. Place on foil-covered cookie sheet and cover carefully with maple syrup. Bake in 350-degree oven until they are brown and tender.

For a fancier version, flambé. Put the cooked apples into a flame-proof bowl. Heat rum—or whatever takes your fancy—in a ladle until it blazes. Pour over apples. They will blaze madly for a bit, then die down. Serve and enjoy.

Russian Cream

An elegant dessert, particularly during fresh berry season.

¾ cup sugar
1 envelope (1 tablespoon) gelatin
½ cup water
1 cup coffee cream
1½ cups sour cream
1 teaspoon vanilla
Fresh berries—raspberries are especially good. You may use frozen, if you like, thawed and seasoned to taste

In saucepan blend sugar and gelatin. Add water and let stand 5 minutes. Bring to a boil, stirring constantly. Remove from heat and pour in cream.

In separate bowl blend sour cream and vanilla. Gradually add hot sugar mixture to cold sour cream mixture and blend well. Pour into individual dishes or into a 1-quart mold. Chill at least 4 hours. Serve with berries. Serves 4–5.

Steamed Cranberry Pudding

½ cup molasses
2 teaspoons baking soda
½ cup boiling water
1⅓ cups flour
2 cups fresh cranberries

Mix together the molasses, soda, and water. Be sure the water is boiling! Toss berries in a bit of flour to coat them. Add flour, then cranberries, in that order, to the molasses mixture. Pour pudding into mold, cover tightly with foil, and tie string around foil. Steam for 2 hours in steamer or on a rack in a large kettle with a closely fitting lid. Serves 4.

Serve with *Sauce Gorgeous:*

½ cup sugar
½ cup cream
¼ cup butter

Stir ingredients together in top of double boiler and cook over hot water for 15 minutes. Serve warm over warm pudding.

Figgy Pudding

This is a wonderful, rich, festive pudding. It is, however, quite a project. Here are a few tips to make the job a little easier. Locate dried figs. Have the butcher grind the suet for you. Also, locate a mold beforehand. It must have a tight fitting cover. We used an old rounded 2½-quart mold with aluminum foil, doubled and held tight with a rubber band, as a cover. You could use 2 coffee cans. The mold or molds must fit into a large kettle for steaming and sit on a trivet to keep them off the bottom.

This recipe will serve 20 or more people.

1¾ cups fresh bread crumbs (use only a high-quality white bread
   and remove the crust)
1½ pounds dried figs
2½ cups milk
2 cups sifted all-purpose flour (sift before measuring)
3 teaspoons baking powder
1¼ cups sugar
1¼ teaspoons ground cinnamon
1¼ teaspoons ground nutmeg
¾ teaspoon salt
5 eggs
1¾ cups ground suet
⅓ cup grated orange peel
3 tablespoons brandy for flaming

Grease mold(s) well. Be sure there is a tight-fitting cover. Make bread crumbs in a food processor using an on-off technique.

Remove stems from figs and chop them in the food processor. Combine figs and milk in a pan and cook, covered, over medium heat for 25 minutes. Cool.

Sift flour, baking powder, sugar, cinnamon, nutmeg, and salt together and set aside.

In large mixer bowl, beat the eggs until light and fluffy. With a sturdy spoon, beat in the fig mixture, flour mixture, suet, bread crumbs and orange peel. Beat until well combined.

Turn into the prepared mold and cover tightly. Place mold on a trivet in a large kettle and add boiling water to come up ¾ of the mold. Steam, covered, for 2½ hours. Check water from time to time and add more when needed. Cool.

Gently remove pudding from mold (if you have trouble with the coffee can molds you may have to remove the bottom and push it out. Flame if desired. (To flame gently heat 3 tablespoons brandy in a small pan just until vapor rises. Ignite with a match and pour over pudding.) Serve warm with hard sauce.

Hard Sauce:

½ cup softened butter
1½ cups powdered sugar
½ teaspoon vanilla extract
2 tablespoons brandy

In the small bowl of the electric mixer, cream butter. Gradually beat in sugar until combined. Stir in the rest of the ingredients and store, covered, in the refrigerator.

Here's the good news — everything can be made in advance. The pudding keeps well and may even be frozen.

Upside-Down Cherry Puffs

2 cups canned sour cherries, drained and juice reserved
¾ teaspoon almond extract
1 tablespoon lemon juice
⅓ cup shortening
Dash of salt
⅔ cup sugar
1 egg, unbeaten
1½ teaspoons baking powder
1 cup flour
⅓ cup milk

Preheat oven to 375 degrees. Butter 6 custard cups. Blend cherries, ¼ teaspoon almond extract, and lemon juice. Divide among prepared custard cups.

Cream shortening, salt, and ½ teaspoon almond extract. Add sugar gradually, beating until mixture is fluffy. Add egg and mix well. Sift baking powder and flour together and add to creamed mixture alternately with milk. Divide batter evenly among custard cups and bake for 30–35 minutes.

To serve, invert into individual dessert dishes while warm and pour a little cherry sauce over each. Garnish with cream if you wish.

Cherry Sauce:

Boil 1 cup reserved cherry juice with ½ cup sugar for 10 minutes. Serves 6.

Blueberry Kuchen

2 cups flour
2 tablespoons sugar
½ cup butter or margarine
1 tablespoon white vinegar
5–6 cups cleaned, fresh blueberries
⅔ cup sugar
2 tablespoons flour
⅛–¼ teaspoon cinnamon

Stir together 2 cups flour and 2 tablespoons sugar. Cut in ½ cup shortening until mixture develops a crumb-like texture. Add vinegar and gather dough into a ball, mixing ingredients well. Press dough into a 9-inch cake pan or springform pan, ¼ inch on bottom and up the sides.

Pour 3 cups blueberries into crust and cover with ⅔ cup sugar mixed with 2 tablespoons flour and cinnamon. Bake at 400 degrees for about 50 minutes, but watch carefully toward end. Crust should be brown and berries bubbling.

Remove from oven and pour over all 2–3 more cups blueberries. Cool. Serve with whipped cream if you like. Serves 8–10.

Apple Goodie

¾ cup sugar
1 tablespoon flour
⅛ teaspoon salt
½ teaspoon cinnamon
2 cups peeled, sliced apples
½ cup rolled oats
½ cup flour
½ cup brown sugar
⅛ teaspoon baking powder
⅛ teaspoon baking soda
4 tablespoons butter

Mix first 5 ingredients, and spread evenly over bottom of well-greased baking dish.

Mix together the rolled oats, flour, brown sugar, baking powder and baking soda. Cut in butter with pastry blender or 2 knives. Spread this mixture evenly over apples. Bake in 375-degree oven for 35 minutes. Serves 4–5.

Apple orchards thrive along Lake Champlain where you can pick your own in fall. McIntosh is the most popular variety.

Lemon-Rosemary Apple Cobbler

You won't believe how good this is until you try it.

Filling:

½ teaspoon dried rosemary leaves
⅓ cup granulated sugar
2 tablespoons freshly squeezed lemon juice
1½ pounds apples, peeled, cored and thinly sliced (5 cups)
Grated rind of half a lemon

Heat oven to 450 degrees. Have ready a heavy dish, a 9-inch pie plate, or a single cake layer pan.

Crush the rosemary as fine as possible. Place in a large bowl. Add sugar, lemon juice, and rind. Stir to mix. Add apples, stirring to coat. Arrange in baking dish.

Topping:

1 cup all-purpose flour
1 tablespoon granulated sugar
1 teaspoon baking powder
⅛ teaspoon salt
½ teaspoon dried rosemary leaves, crushed as fine as possible
3 tablespoons cold, unsalted butter, cut up
⅓ cup light cream or milk

Mix dry ingredients into medium-sized bowl. Add butter and cut in with pastry blender or knives until mixture is the consistency of coarse cornmeal. Add cream or milk and stir until a soft dough forms. Knead on lightly floured surface 10–12 times. Roll to fit baking dish, place over apples, seal edges, and cut slits. Bake 25–30 minutes, until golden. Serve warm with cream. Serves 6.

There are 3 medium-sized apples to a pound. Three pounds of apples make 9 cups of slices and 4 cups of applesauce.

Fresh Strawberries in Wine with Ginger

1½ quarts strawberries, hulled and halved
1 cup powdered sugar, or to taste
½ teaspoon pumpkin pie spice
1 teaspoon grated lemon peel
1 cup port wine, or other sweet wine
Whipped cream, lightly sweetened
Candied ginger, chopped fine

Sift powdered sugar over prepared strawberries to desired sweetness. Combine spice, lemon peel, and wine, and pour over berries, mixing gently. Let marinate 2 hours.

At serving time, whip the cream and pour into a serving dish. Place berries and chopped ginger each in its own serving bowl. Pass the three, allowing each person to help himself to berries and cream, garnished with ginger. Serves 8.

Strawberries ripen by late June in Vermont, just in time for making strawberry shortcake on the Fourth of July.

Strawberry Rhubarb Flummery

1 quart frozen or fresh rhubarb, cut in pieces
1 package frozen strawberries, or 2 pints fresh, hulled
1 cup light brown sugar
½ cup water
2 tablespoons cornstarch
Dash of salt

Put all ingredients in a saucepan. Stirring constantly, bring slowly to a boil. Boil 1 minute. Pour into bowl and refrigerate. To serve, top with whipped cream. Serves 6–8.

Almond Baked Apples

¼ cup sugar
¼ cup butter or margarine
1 tablespoon flour
1 tablespoon milk
1 cup sliced almonds
1 teaspoon vanilla
6 medium, tart apples, peeled, cored, and halved

Preheat oven to 425 degrees. Grease a baking dish large enough to hold apple halves close together in 1 layer. In a small saucepan over medium heat, stir sugar, butter, flour, and milk until butter melts and mixture is well blended. Remove from heat and stir in almonds and vanilla. Set aside.

Place apple halves, rounded side up, in baking dish. Top each half with about 1 tablespoon of almond mixture. Bake until apples are tender and almond mixture is golden brown—about 15–20 minutes. Serve slightly warm, with whipped cream if desired. Serves 12.

Apricot Obsession

Unusual, easy, and very good.

1 pound dried apricots
6 ounces brown sugar
½ cup broken walnut meats
6 tablespoons butter
¾ cup flour
¼ cup sugar
Pinch of salt

Heat oven to 400 degrees. Wash and separate apricots. Simmer in enamel pan with walnuts, just covered with hot water. When nearly cooked, add brown sugar and stir carefully. Try not to let apricots get mushy. When it looks like jam, turn into a bake-and-serve dish. Combine butter, flour, sugar and salt until crumbly. Sprinkle over apricots. Bake for 20 minutes, then chill. Serve with whipped cream. Serves 6–8.

Fresh Fruit and . . .

Some thoughts about serving fresh fruit in ways equal to the most elegant dinner party. First, combine with an eye to color as well as taste. For example:

Melon balls with blueberries or blackberries
The above combinations with peeled, sliced kiwi fruit
Fresh, ripe peaches with blueberries
Strawberries, kiwis and blueberries

And so on. Now, what to do with fruit mixtures?

Let stand in white wine for a while.
Let stand in a combination of white wine and orange juice.
Let stand in combination of white wine, gingerale, and fresh lime juice.
Let stand in fresh orange juice.

Add Grand Marnier, Triple Sec, or some such, to any of above mixtures. Sprinkle with toasted coconut just before serving.

Add a dollop of low-fat, fruit-flavored yogurt—lemon looks and tastes especially good.

Don't forget fresh mint—a sprig tucked in each dish looks festive.

And last, but far from least, try sprinkling the fruit with lime or lemon zest (rind) and sugar, thusly:

Using a vegetable peeler or a "zester," remove the thinnest colored layer of rind from either a lemon or a lime. Avoid the white layer as it is very bitter. Then slice into thin strips with a sharp knife. Mash these slivers into 2–3 tablespoons granulated sugar, using the back of a spoon or a mortar and pestle, until sugar takes on the color of the zest and absorbs it. Sprinkle over fresh fruit, add a spoonful of yogurt, and enjoy.

Cold Pineapple-Orange Fruit Compote

Either a dessert or a refreshing accompaniment for roast meat or poultry, this is a lovely addition to a buffet table.

1 large fresh pineapple, peeled, cored and cubed
6 oranges, peeled, sectioned, membranes and seeds removed, cubed
½ cup powdered sugar
¼ cup orange-flavored liqueur
1 cup toasted coconut (toast on cookie sheet in 350-degree oven,
    stirring often, for about 8 minutes)

Mix all ingredients together except coconut, and place in refrigerator, covered. Stir several times. Sprinkle with coconut just before serving. Serves 12.

Chocolate Coconut Bars

Mix and bake right in the pan—easy, quick, delicious!

8 tablespoons margarine or butter, melted in 9- x 13-inch pan
1½ cups graham cracker crumbs
½–1 teaspoon cinnamon
1 (6 ounce) package semisweet chocolate bits
1 (3½ ounce) can flaked coconut (about 1¼ cups)
1 cup chopped walnuts
1 can sweetened condensed milk

Preheat oven to 350 degrees. To melted butter in your baking pan add crumbs and cinnamon and mix well. Press evenly onto pan bottom to form crust. Sprinkle chocolate bits, then coconut, then nuts, evenly over crust. Pour condensed milk over all. Bake for 25 minutes or until lightly browned.

Filled Raisin Cookies

A Vermont classic.

Dough:

1 cup sugar
½ cup shortening
1 egg
1 teaspoon vanilla
3½ cups flour
3 teaspoons baking powder
1 teaspoon baking soda
½ teaspoon salt
½ cup milk

Blend sugar, shortening, egg and vanilla; mix well. Sift dry ingredients together and add alternately to creamed mixture with milk. Beat to make smooth dough.

Filling:

2 cups seedless raisins put through food chopper or processor
1 cup sugar
2 teaspoons flour
1 cup water

Boil ingredients slowly for 10 minutes. Let cool.

To assemble:

Preheat oven to 350 degrees and grease cookie sheets. Roll dough ¼-inch thick and cut with cookie cutter into circles. Put 1 heaping teaspoon of raisin filling on 1 circle. Top with another circle which has been pricked with a fork. Press edges of circles together and place on cookie sheets. Bake 15–20 minutes.

Lumberjacks

This recipe makes 4 dozen large, soft cookies. The dough keeps indefinitely in the refrigerator.

1 cup sugar
1 cup shortening
1 cup dark molasses
2 eggs
4 cups sifted flour
1 teaspoon soda
1 teaspoon salt
2 teaspoons cinnamon
1 teaspoon ground ginger

Cream sugar and shortening. Add molasses and unbeaten eggs. Mix well. Sift together the dry ingredients and stir in.

Put ¼ cup granulated sugar in a small bowl. Dip fingers into sugar, then pinch off a ball of dough the size of a walnut. Dip into sugar. Place on greased cookie sheet about 3 inches apart. Bake at 350 degrees for 12–15 minutes.

Sweets

Chocolate Chip Kisses

This is a recipe from "Aunt Marion" who ran a tea room called The Golden Pheasant in downtown Burlington in the 20's and 30's. She went to the Fannie Farmer Cooking School and this was one of her best-loved recipes.

2 egg whites
⅛ teaspoon salt
⅛ teaspoon cream of tartar
¾ cup sugar
1 (6 ounce) package chocolate chips
½ teaspoon vanilla

Preheat oven to 300 degrees. Line cookie sheets with ungreased brown paper.

Beat egg whites until frothy. Add salt and cream of tartar and beat until stiff but not dry. Continue beating while adding sugar, 2 tablespoons at a time. Fold in chocolate chips and vanilla. Drop by the teaspoonful onto the prepared cookie sheets and bake for 25 minutes, or until light brown and dry. Remove from paper while warm.

Possible variations: Use peppermint extract in place of vanilla. Add candied cherries and nuts along with chocolate chips.

Apricot Surprise

⅔ cup sweetened condensed milk
2 cups flaked coconut
Dash of salt
1 cup chopped dried apricots

Preheat oven to 350 degrees and grease cookie sheets. Combine all ingredients and form into small balls. Bake on prepared sheets about 12 minutes or until lightly browned. Remove from cookie sheet at once. Makes about 2 dozen.

Date Nut Squares

2 eggs
½ cup sugar
½ teaspoon vanilla
½ cup flour
½ teaspoon baking powder
½ teaspoon salt
1 cup chopped walnuts
2 cups finely chopped dates

Preheat oven to 325 degrees and grease well an 8- x 8- x 2-inch pan. Beat eggs until foamy. Beat in sugar and vanilla. Sift dry ingredients together and stir into eggs. Mix in nuts and dates. Spread in prepared pan and bake about 25–30 minutes—until top has a dull crust. Cut into squares while warm, sprinkle with powdered sugar, and remove from pan when cool. Makes 16 2-inch squares.

Mom's Oatmeal and Date Squares

A holiday favorite—stores well in a cookie tin.

Crust:

4 cups quick-cooking rolled oats
4 cups sifted white flour
4 cups brown sugar
2 cups margarine, melted
2 teaspoons baking soda
Optional: ½ teaspoon cinnamon and 1 cup chopped nuts

In a large bowl, combine all ingredients. Mix well.

Filling:

1 pound pitted dates, cut fine
2 cups brown sugar
2 cups water
Grated rind of 1 lemon (optional)

Cook ingredients in saucepan until thick, approximately one hour.

To assemble:

Preheat oven to 350 degrees. Spread half of crust mixture on an ungreased cookie sheet and pat down firmly. Spread filling mix evenly over this. Top with remaining half of crust mixture and press down gently all over. Bake 25–30 minutes, until edges are brown. Makes 72 small squares.

Pecan Logs

1 cup butter, softened
¾ cup sugar
1 egg
1 teaspoon almond extract
3 cups flour
½ teaspoon nutmeg
½ cup sugar
1½ cups chopped pecans
2 egg whites

Preheat oven to 375 degrees. Grease cookie sheets. Beat butter until light. Add ¾ cup sugar and continue beating until fluffy. Beat in egg and almond extract.

Sift together flour and nutmeg and stir into creamed mixture. Shape dough into rolls about 2 inches long and ½ inch in diameter.

Combine the ½ cup sugar with chopped nuts. Beat egg whites slightly. Dip logs into egg whites, then roll in nut mixture. Place on greased cookie sheets and bake for about 10 minutes. Remove and cool on racks. Makes about 6 dozen cookies.

Chocolate Christmas Bars

1½ cups flour
1½ teaspoons cinnamon
1 teaspoon ground cloves
¼ teaspoon allspice
½ teaspoon baking soda
2 squares unsweetened chocolate
2 eggs
1½ cups packed brown sugar
¼ cup honey
½ cup chopped citron
½ pound slivered almonds or ¼ teaspoon almond extract

Preheat oven to 350 degrees and line a 9- x 13-inch pan with waxed paper.

Sift flour, spices, and soda together and set aside. Grate chocolate and set aside. Beat eggs until frothy. Add sugar gradually while continuing to beat until mixture is creamy. Stir in grated chocolate. Add flour combination alternately with honey. Stir in citron and almonds. Spoon into prepared pan and even off the top. Bake 35–40 minutes or until cake pulls away from sides of pan. Remove from pan; gently peel off paper. When completely cool spread with Chocolate Butter Frosting (page 254) and cut into little bars. Makes about 4 dozen 3- x ¾-inch bars.

Dutch-process chocolate contains more sodium than milk chocolate.

Chocolate Butter Frosting

1 square bitter chocolate
1 tablespoon butter
2 tablespoons hot water
Pinch of salt
½ teaspoon vanilla
1 cup powdered sugar

Melt chocolate and butter. Stir in water and salt. Cool. Stir in vanilla and sugar until spreadable. Spread evenly over cooled Chocolate Christmas Bars.

English Lace Cookies

1 cup oatmeal
1 cup sugar (may use half dark brown for richer flavor)
1 egg, beaten
8 tablespoons margarine, melted
1 teaspoon vanilla
3 tablespoons flour
1 teaspoon baking powder
1 teaspoon salt

Heat oven to 350 degrees. Mix all ingredients together and drop by teaspoonsful on an aluminum foil-covered cookie sheet. Bake for 8–10 minutes or less—just until cookies begin to turn brown. Wait until completely cool and then peel away foil. If you are in a great hurry, just slide foil off the cookie sheet and lay a new piece down. Makes about 50 cookies.

One way to cope with the removal problem for thin cookies is to line cookie sheet with aluminum foil, grease it, drop cookies onto it, then slide the whole thing off the cookie sheet when baked. Remove foil from cookies when they have cooled rather than cookies from foil.

Butter Chews

An old-fashioned, and very rich, bar cookie. This recipe was a grand-mother's gift to a newly married granddaughter many years ago.

Shortcake:

¾ cup butter
3 tablespoons granulated sugar
1½ cups flour

Preheat oven to 375 degrees. Cream butter and sugar together until creamy and smooth. Blend in flour and pat mixture into bottom of greased 9- x 9 inch pan. Bake for 15 minutes or until lightly browned.

Topping:

3 eggs, separated
2 cups brown sugar
1 cup chopped nuts
¾ cup coconut
Powdered sugar

Beat egg yolks until foamy, then add brown sugar and beat well. Add nuts and coconut. Beat egg whites until stiff but not dry and fold into yolk mixture. Pour this over shortcake just after you remove it from the oven. Return to oven and bake for 25–30 minutes. Dust with powdered sugar and cut when cooled a bit.

Oatmeal Applesauce Cookies

¾ cup butter or margarine
1½ cups sugar (you may want to use less if applesauce is sweetened)
2 eggs
1 cup applesauce
1 teaspoon vanilla
1¾ cups flour
2 teaspoons baking powder
½ teaspoon baking soda
½ teaspoon salt
1 teaspoon cinnamon
½ teaspoon nutmeg
¼ teaspoon cloves
2 cups rolled oats
½ to 1 cup raisins

Preheat oven to 375 degrees and grease baking sheets. Cream butter and sugar until light. Beat in eggs. Add applesauce and vanilla. Sift together the flour, baking powder, soda, salt and spices, and stir into creamed mixture. Add oats and raisins. Drop by teaspoonsful onto prepared baking sheets. Bake for 12 minutes or so. Makes 5½ dozen.

A soft, slightly chewy cookie—very flavorful.

If raisins dry out in the box, sprinkle them (in box) with several drops of water, wrap in plastic wrap and microwave on high for 10–15 seconds. They will revive.

5-in-1 Tea Cookies

An old-time family favorite. The sugar cookie dough will keep for weeks in the refrigerator, and to make up a batch of different cookies, change the add-ins.

2 cups butter
2 cups sugar
1 cup brown sugar
4 eggs
3 teaspoons cream of tartar
6½ cups flour
2 teaspoons baking soda
¼ cup milk

Cream the butter and sugars until smooth and fluffy. (For plain sugar cookies add 2 teaspoons vanilla). Stir in eggs, 1 at a time. Mix together flour, cream of tartar, and baking soda, then add alternately with milk to the creamed mixture. Mix thoroughly. This makes 8 cups of dough. Refrigerate, then bake cookies as needed on buttered cookie sheet in 375-degree oven 10–15 minutes.

1. *Chocolate Bits:* mix into 1 cup cookie dough, 1 tablespoon cocoa and ⅓ cup chocolate chips. Shape about 2 dozen round balls.

2. *Ginger:* Stir into 1 cup cookie dough 1 tablespoon molasses and ⅓ teaspoon ginger. Shape about 24 balls. Dip fingers in water so dough doesn't stick to hands.

3. *Fruit 'n' Spice:* Stir into 1 cup cookie dough ½ cup cooked and drained dried fruit, 2 tablespoons brown sugar, ¼ teaspoon cinnamon, ⅛ teaspoon cloves. Drop by teaspoonsful onto cookie sheet. Makes 36.

4. *Orange:* Stir into 1 cup cookie dough ¼ cup grated orange peel and ¼ cup sugar mixed with 4 teaspoons orange juice. Bake as drop cookies. Makes 24.

5. *Gum Drop:* Mix into 1 cup cookie dough ½ cup gum drops cut fine. Shape into 24 balls, criss-cross with fork.

All-Time Favorite Oatmeal Cookies

2 cups quick or old-fashioned rolled oats
2 cups all-purpose flour
1 teaspoon baking soda
1 teaspoon salt
1 teaspoon cinnamon
1 cup butter or margarine, room temperature
1 cup firmly packed brown sugar
1 teaspoon vanilla
2 eggs, room temperature
1½ cups of one of the following:
   chopped candied fruit (fruit cake mix)
   dried mixed fruit bits
   dried apricots, chopped and mixed with a sprinkle of flour
½ cup raisins
1 cup chopped nuts

Preheat oven to 350 degrees and lightly grease 2 cookie sheets. Stir together the oats, flour, soda, salt, and cinnamon. Set aside. Cream butter, sugar, and vanilla together, and beat until light. Add eggs, 1 at a time, beating after each. Gradually add oat mixture, combining well.

Add fruits and nuts by hand. Drop by teaspoonsful onto prepared cookie sheet and bake 9–10 minutes. Do not overbake—they will firm up as they cool. Makes about 5½ dozen.

Accompaniments

Dilly Onion Rings

These onion rings are good with beef and on meat sandwiches. They keep indefinitely in your refrigerator.

1 large mild onion, sliced thin and separated into rings
½ cup sugar
2 teaspoons salt
1 teaspoon dried dillweed
½ cup white vinegar
¼ cup water

Combine sugar, salt, dill, vinegar, and water, stirring to dissolve sugar. Pour over onion rings. Cover and refrigerate overnight, stirring occasionally.

Dutch Tomato Relish

A great recipe for that late-summer glut of fast-ripening tomatoes. Cut the good parts of those which are going too fast, and weigh them on your bathroom scales—it will take a full, large mixing bowl.

7 pounds ripe tomatoes
3 pounds sugar (7½ cups)
Vinegar
2 tablespoons whole cloves

Remove peels from tomatoes, cut in chunks, place in large bowl, and cover with vinegar. Top bowl with a dinner plate and leave overnight.

Next day, put tomatoes in a colander and let them drain while you do other early-morning chores. After a while put them in a kettle with sugar and the cloves which have been tied in a cheesecloth bag. Simmer without cover for 2 or 3 hours, until thickish. Pour into jars and cover with paraffin.

Rhubarb Chutney

8 cups rhubarb cut in ½-inch pieces
2 cups chopped apples (peeled)
1½ cups raisins
1 tablespoon crushed dried red pepper
2 medium cloves garlic, minced
1 cup chopped onion
½ cup cider vinegar
3 cups dark brown sugar, firmly packed
1 jar (2.7 ounces) crystallized ginger, minced
1 teaspoon cinnamon
1 teaspoon cloves
¼ teaspoon nutmeg
¼ teaspoon allspice
1 teaspoon salt

Combine all ingredients in a large stainless steel or enamel pot, bring to a boil and simmer for about 2½ hours, stirring occasionally to be sure the bottom doesn't burn. When the consistency is right, ladle into hot, sterilized jars and seal immediately.

Cranberry Kumquat Maple Conserve

12 fresh kumquats, unpeeled, sliced thin and seeds removed
1 pound fresh cranberries, washed and drained
¾ cup medium-amber Vermont maple syrup

In a saucepan combine all ingredients and bring to a simmer over medium heat. When berries begin to pop, reduce heat to low, cover, and cook, stirring from time to time, about 8–10 minutes.

Uncover, raise heat, and cook, stirring constantly, until mixture becomes thick—about 2 or 3 minutes. Makes about 3 cups.

Cranberry Chutney Conserve

A nice twist on the usual cranberry sauce. It is an elegant accompaniment to the holiday turkey, to a roast duck, or to a curry dish.

1 bag (1 pound) fresh cranberries
3–4 tablespoons butter
½ cup sugar, approximately
Pinch of salt
2 tablespoons brandy or sherry
1 jar premium-brand chutney (mango-pepper is particularly good)

Coarsely chop cranberries in food processor. Combine them with butter, sugar, and salt in a saucepan, and cook over medium heat until mixture begins to thicken. Add brandy or sherry and chutney. Continue to cook over low heat until well-blended and thickened.

Church bazaars crowd the calendar in summer and the Christmas season. They are prime places to find homemade pickles, breads, jellies, and relishes arrayed in jewel colors in little glass jars.

Boiled Cider

From a cookbook committee member:

"A native Vermonter, I had managed to get through over half a century without tasting boiled cider. I didn't know what I was missing! It was mentioned as a logical inclusion in this book, so the search was on for a recipe. To no avail. I figured that boiled cider must be just that, so I poured 1 gallon fresh apple cider into a large stainless steel stockpot and boiled it.

"Here's my method: Bring cider to a rolling boil and then turn down to a good simmer so that it continues to evaporate. You can then go about your business and forget about it for a few hours. I simmered mine for about 5 hours, or until it was syrupy. No trick to it—just simmer it until it achieves a consistency that pleases you. It has a wonderful, tart, apple taste, and is a surprising treat on a number of things."

Try this on Puffy Pancake, Cottage Cheese Pancakes, apple pie or custard pie, for starters. And the pièce de résistance is a dollop on top of the hard sauce on top of the Figgy Pudding!

The cider mills that dot the roadsides of rural Vermont sell fresh cider all year, turning fall's bounty into a refreshing drink whether served cold or spicy-hot.

To make hot mulled cider drop into a quart of cider a cheesecloth bag or tea ball filled with ½ teaspoon whole allspice, ½ teaspoon whole cloves, and 2 broken sticks of cinnamon. Simmer 15 minutes, remove spices, and enjoy in front of the crackling fire.

Stewed Apples or Pears

Serve this dish for a lovely accompaniment to turkey, chicken, or roast pork.

3 pounds firm, flavorful apples or firm pears
3 tablespoons butter
⅔ cup sugar
⅔ cup water
⅔ cup sauterne
1 piece lemon peel
4 tablespoons lemon juice

Peel and core apples. Cut in thick slices. Sauté slices in butter about 5 minutes and sprinkle with sugar. Add remaining ingredients to skillet and simmer until apples are tender.

Garlic Olive Oil

If you love garlic, this is definitely for you. Easy to do and to keep on hand, it is useful and delicious in a variety of ways.

1 (8 ounce) bottle virgin olive oil (a big bottle makes more sense here)
10 cloves garlic, peeled

Put garlic cloves in olive oil, cap, and let stand for about a week. Check intensity of flavor and if you want more, add more garlic.

Possible uses include:

1. Salad dressings, of course

2. Baked potatoes: Rub washed baking potatoes with garlic oil and sprinkle generously with fresh-ground pepper. Bake as usual.

3. Corn on the cob: Pull back husks, brush ears with garlic oil, pull husks back up over ears, and cook on the grill.

Pesto

The basic unit of measurement in this recipe is "2 cups fresh basil leaves."
Measure by packing with moderate firmness. You may multiply or divide
both the basil and the other ingredients proportionately if you want to vary
your final quantity. This recipe will make enough pesto sauce for pasta for 2.

2 cups basil leaves
Olive oil

Place basil in blender or processor and process with just enough olive oil to
make a smooth paste. At this point, you may pack in a container and freeze.
When you want to serve it, either thaw this mixture, or continue right along
by adding:

2 cloves garlic
¼ cup pine nuts
¼ cup Parmesan cheese
Pinch of salt, if desired
Olive oil as needed

Blend or process these ingredients with the basil mixture to make a smooth
paste. Use at this point on bluefish or other fish. Add a tablespoon or so of
hot water to make sauce for pasta.

Low-Fat Salad Dressing

The amounts given in the recipe are sufficient for 1 salad. The dressing can be made in any quantity by keeping the proportions the same: 3 parts oil to 1 part vinegar and substituting low-fat yogurt for ⅓ of the oil if you wish.

1 teaspoon Dijon-style mustard
1 clove garlic, crushed
1 teaspoon (more or less) fresh herbs of your choice, chopped
Salt and pepper
1 tablespoon red wine vinegar
3 tablespoons olive oil *or* 2 tablespoons oil and 1 tablespoon low-fat yogurt

Combine all ingredients and whip until creamy.

To make your own fromage blanc, or yogurt cheese, drain plain low-fat yogurt without added gelatin overnight through double-thick cheesecloth. Drain 16 ounces of yogurt to make 1 cup of yogurt cheese. Use it as a low-fat alternative to cream cheese, sour cream, and heavy cream, letting it come to room temperature before adding to hot mixtures.

Creamy Garlic-Dill Dressing

This dressing is wonderfully flavorful. Mix it up in a screw-top jar, use what you want, and store the rest in the fridge. It keeps for several weeks. It can be thinned (and refreshed) with the addition of a little buttermilk if you wish.

⅓ cup mayonnaise
1 cup low-fat yogurt
1 teaspoon maple syrup
2 teaspoons cider vinegar
2 teaspoons fresh dill, chopped
2 small-to-medium cloves garlic, crushed

Mix all ingredients together. Let stand, covered, in the refrigerator for an hour or so to let flavors blend. Adjust seasonings to your taste. Makes 1½ cups.

French Dressing

Juice of 1½ oranges
Juice of 1½ lemons
1 cup vinegar
1½ cups salad oil
2 tablespoons paprika
¾ cup sugar mixed with 1 tablespoon dry mustard
1 tablespoon salt, more or less
1 tablespoon Worcestershire sauce
1 clove garlic, split

Put all ingredients into a quart jar with a good screw top. Shake well to mix. Stores well in refrigerator. Makes 1 quart.

Maple Syrup and Balsamic Vinegar Dressing

1 teaspoon dry mustard
½ teaspoon dried basil
1 cup extra-virgin olive oil
3 tablespoons balsamic vinegar
1 tablespoon lemon juice
2 tablespoons maple syrup
Salt and freshly ground pepper to taste

Combine mustard and basil in a small bowl. Add olive oil, vinegar, lemon juice, and maple syrup. Beat ingredients together until dressing is emulsified. Adjust seasonings and add salt and pepper to taste. Makes 1 cup dressing, which will keep, covered, in the refrigerator for several weeks.

Sharp Brown Sauce for Ham

¼ cup finely chopped onions
½ cup brown sugar
1 tablespoon flour
½ cup vinegar
1 teaspoon Worcestershire sauce
½ teaspoon salt
Dash of paprika

Combine all ingredients in saucepan, stirring till blended. Cook over low heat, stirring occasionally, until thickened. This will take just a few minutes, and sauce should be carefully watched—it burns easily.

Makes ¾ cup and doubles well.

Mustard Sauce

¼ cup dry mustard
½ cup vinegar
¼ cup sugar
1 egg yolk

Mix mustard and vinegar and let stand at room temperature for about 4 hours.

Mix sugar and egg yolk in sauce pan. Add mustard mixture. Heat till sauce thickens slightly. Cool and serve at room temperature with Spinach Balls (see page 10).

High-flavored condiments like horse-radish add spark to yogurt-based dressings and sauces.

Ski Tea

Just the thing when everybody ends up back at your house after an afternoon of cross-country skiing! This one comes to us from our "mother book," *Out of Vermont Kitchens*, now 50 years young. Some things just never grow old.

25 cups water
1 heaping teaspoon cinnamon
1 heaping teaspoon whole cloves
5 tea bags of Orange Pekoe tea
Juice of 6 oranges
Juice of 3 lemons
1 pound of sugar, or to taste

Measure water into a nonaluminum pot. Tie spices in a small bag and add, along with tea bags, to water. Bring to a boil, turn off heat, and steep for 3 minutes. Remove bags and add juices and sugar. Serve piping hot in punch cups. Serves 50.

To add fresh flavor to frozen orange juice add some juice from a lemon.

Frozen Strawberry Daiquiris

1 (12 ounce) can frozen limeade concentrate, thawed
2½ limeade cans of light rum
3 cans water
6½ cups (frozen) sliced strawberries in syrup, thawed

Combine all ingredients well in a large plastic container. Cover tightly and freeze for at least 12 hours. Just before serving, stir well and place a portion in the blender. Do not add ice. Blend well and serve—it will be slushy. Garnish with whipped cream and fresh berries, if you like. This keeps indefinitely in the freezer.

Lime Sparkler

4 limes
2 cups sugar (superfine if possible)
2 cups water

Grate rinds of limes and set aside. Squeeze limes and strain the juice. In a pan, combine the sugar and water, boiling until the sugar dissolves. Add lime rind. Simmer 10 minutes. Allow to cool to lukewarm, then strain into a jar, pressing on the rind to release its essence. Add lime juice. Now you have about 3 cups of lime syrup which will keep in the refrigerator at least 2 weeks, and which can be used when needed to make refreshing Lime Sparklers.

To make a Sparkler put ice in a large glass. Pour in ¼ cup lime syrup plus the juice of 1 small or ½ medium lime. Then pop the squeezed half of lime right into the glass and fill with seltzer. Stir to mix, and thirst no more.

Sweet Lassi

A refreshing summer drink borrowed from India.

2 cups plain yogurt
2 cups very cold water
3 tablespoons sugar, or to taste
1 teaspoon rose water, available at health food stores (optional)

Mix all ingredients in the blender for several minutes until very frothy. Serve chilled. If stored in the refrigerator, stir before serving. Serves 3–4.

Christmas Champagne Punch

1 pint cranberry juice
1 cup lemon juice
1 (6 ounce) can frozen orange juice
1 cup superfine granulated sugar
1 bottle white wine
2 bottles champagne

Mix juices, sugar, and white wine, combining well until sugar dissolves. At serving time, add champagne. Serves 20.

Sara's Wedding Punch

4 tablespoons sugar
1 tablespoon aromatic bitters
½ cup fresh or frozen lemon juice
1 cup brandy
1 cup orange-flavored liqueur
2 bottles dry champagne, chilled
2 (28 ounce) bottles club soda
Lemon and orange slices for garnish

Combine sugar, bitters, lemon juice, brandy, and liqueur in a punch bowl. Just before serving, add champagne and club soda. Stir to blend. Add ice and garnishes. Makes 30 4-ounce servings.

Cranberry Punch

To 1 gallon cranberry juice, add 5 sticks cinnamon. Let sit for 2 or 3 days and serve either hot or cold.

Sangria

This is great for a large gathering. It is best made ahead to allow flavors to blend and deepen. Strain it at serving time.

½ gallon burgundy—cheap is fine, particularly if you are going
    to let it sit for a while
1 (6 ounce) can frozen orange juice, undiluted
⅛ cup lemon juice
⅛ cup lime juice
¼ cup sugar, or to taste
2 cups lemon-lime soda
½ cup brandy—cheap is fine
½ cup canned peaches, soaked overnight in burgundy
Orange slices to float on top at serving time

Put 1 cup or 2 of burgundy into blender, add sugar, and process to get sugar into solution. Frozen orange juice can be added at this time.

Combine all ingredients in a suitable container and let stand as long as possible. At serving time, taste, and add whatever seems right to you. Strain into punch bowl or pitcher and garnish with thin orange slices.

Vermont Whiskey Sour

5 ounces orange juice
5 ounces lemon juice
10 ounces blended whiskey
¼ cup maple syrup—amber if you can get it

Put all ingredients in a blender and turn it on high. With the motor running, drop in 8–10 ice cubes. Serve over ice. Yields 4 servings.

Note: You can add more or less syrup to suit your taste.

The shelf life of coffee is increased if stored in the freezer. Whole beans can be kept for 6 months in a zip-lock plastic bag.

Richmond, Vt

Special Thanks

We would like to thank the many friends, both within and without the Diocese of Vermont, who have helped make this book possible. We hope we've acknowledged everyone who has made a contribution, and are truly sorry for any possible omission.

Cathy Ahlers
Elizabeth Alexander
Marilynn S. Alexander
Sandy Attridge
The Rev. Gordon Bardos
Martha Beatty
Lari Beck
The Rev. Polly Beebe-Bove
Mrs. Arthur E. Bello
Mrs. Donald Blackmer
Anne Brown
Ann Burroughs
Carolyn Butterfield
Sophie Canelake
Ann Carlson
Barbara Champlin
Jean Chase
Guy Cheng
Dorothy Curtis
Dorothy Darling
Nancy Davidson
Estelle Deane
Priscilla Dugan
Dot Evans
Claudia Fischer
Geneva Foote
Kaaren Foss
Francis Foster
Bonnie Fournier
Doris Gilleland
Ellen Gillies

Virginia Golodetz
Billie Griggs
Robert Haggarty
Priscilla Hall
Sue Halvosa
Harriet Hand
Drew Hannah
Sherrill Harbison
Charles and Isabel Hartenbach
Dawn Hazelett
Christine Hemenway
Irene Hendee
Mary Henderson
Hilda Hendrickson
Diane Herberg
Kathryn Herberg
Barbara Jane Hill
Grace Hill
Chips Holden
Bruce Howden
The Rev. DeW. Halsey Howe
Clarinda Irish
Gayle Jacobson
Judy Jay
Kay Johnson
Ron Kallinger
Anne Kennison
The Rev. Dr. Driss R. Knickerbocker
Anne Knowlton
Ida Krasofski
Constance S. Kurth

Peter Kurth
Sara Lascelles
Liz Lauritzen
Sawyer Lee
Elaine Little
Mary Macomber
Mary Barbara Maher
Priscilla March
Margaret Maurice
Mabel W. Mayforth
Shirley Mayforth
Sara McCulloch
John McDonald
Patricia Mcdonald
Vern McDonald, Champlain College
Allan McIlvaine
The Rev. Jeanette McKnight
Gladys Merriman
Elizabeth Metcalfe
Lee Monro
Barbara Moore
Louise Mounsey
Stella Moyser
Julia Northrup
Terry Osmun
Alice D. Outwater
Amanda Parker
Nancy Parkhill
Margaret Parlour
The Rev. Cora Partridge
Jennifer Pastore
Derk Pereboom
Nancy Perkins
Dennis Phillips
Judy Phillips
Leigh Phillips
Keith and Penny Pillsbury
Annagret Pollard
Elizabeth Post
Polly Premo
David Prouty
Stephen Rainville
Janet Raymond

Mary Reath
The Rev. Deborah Rice
Sylvia Rich
Norma Rigby
Carolyn Rood
Janet Rood
Gertrude Rouleau
Debbie Salomon
Carol Sankowski
Abbe Sawabini
Adele Scaccia-White
Kit Serrell
The Rev. Karen Sheldon
Colleen Shover
Gloria Singer
David and Willie Smith
The Rt. Rev. John Smith
Linda Sparks
Paige Stackpole
Joann Stanfield
Marilyn Stout
Mary Stuart
Jean Sturges
Sally Swenson
Edith Templin
Johanna Thomas
Mrs. P.W. Toth
Kirk Trabant
Mary Tuthill
Beverly Vail
Mary Veino
Mrs. James H. Viele
Barbara Wadhams
Helen Wafler
Carol and David Walters
Beverly Watson
Dinny Weed
Carlene Whitcomb
Susan White
Tony Williams
Alice Winn
Priscilla Wohl

Index